# WESTFALL

A Novel

Matthew T. Baker

## Acknowledgements

To the many people who read this is book in manuscript form, the suggestions, insight, and support were invaluable. Thank you all for your time, inspiration, and encouragement.

Special thanks to, Selene Ahn, Randi Kent, Melissa Pritchard, Alison Stout, Robert and Carol Baker, and especially Betsy Rosenmiller, for all their love and generous support during the writing of this novel.

To my late Uncle, Charles Seaver I send my love and gratitude for the inspiration to write this book, and the inspiration to live deliberately.

*For Charles Seaver*

I grasp the hands of those next to me, and take my place in the ring to suffer and to work, taught by instinct, that so shall the dumb abyss be vocal with speech.

Emerson

Prologue

Westfall Academy, in the Town of Westfall outside Boston

Δ   Δ   Δ

Oliver recovered from surgery in time for graduation, and by then I both revered and feared him with more intensity than ever before. Everyone at school thought they understood what losing his left eye had meant to Oliver as a painter. But they didn't know, nor could they, and perhaps because I didn't pretend to understand his loss he allowed me near him when he pushed everyone else away. All I knew were the facts, and at times, how he felt about them.

It happened on a sunny Friday in March, during a noontime cookout held on the expansive lawn that lay like green velvet between the white colonial school buildings. It was the first day of spring, and thus, with youthful fervor a small food fight erupted and quickly developed into a full scale war involving chicken wings, hot-dogs, Boston Baked Beans, apples, ice-cream, everything and anything that could instantly be turned into a viable projectile. It happened in the way these things do, without any one person shouldering full responsibility for it. Oliver was walking with his accustomed long legged grace across the green through the mass of students while all edible stock were in flight around him. He was as always, oblivious, unaware, or even, it seemed, immune to the action of life. Then, suddenly, he was hit. It was an accident, of course--no one meant for Oliver, the school's most gifted artist, to suffer. The next day, in the all-school assembly, I listened to how everyone was to blame, how everyone was responsible for the accident since no one had seen who threw the watermelon rind at Oliver and no one had come forward to claim responsibility for the act. I sat in my wooden chair with my head lowered like everyone else, listening in disbelief, and filled with anger and shame.

When the watermelon rind made contact with his eye Oliver fainted. The pain, the Doctor said, had sent him immediately into shock. Oliver said he never felt any pain, there was only the short moment of surprise and then a peculiar sound, a dull thud, as if an enormous oak door had suddenly closed somewhere near by.

Severe corneal abrasion and a punctured globe are what sent him to the Westfall Hospital emergency room. He had immediate surgery. Dr. Finn gave him an injection of inert gas to keep the globe spherical and flatten the retina. All this put him on his stomach in the school infirmary for three weeks (if he had stood up or rolled over the eye would have slid until he was looking into the top of his head). The glaucoma, or swelling in the eye, was expected, but after two and a half weeks on his stomach complications set in. The retina, all 17 tissue paper thin layers, detached while he was asleep and he was in for blindness. Dr. Finn wanted to try and save Oliver's sight, but finally the glaucoma won out and Oliver insisted he have the final operation. Dr. Finn wanted more time, but Oliver seemed to know he was going to lose the battle. He went back to the hospital and in two hours (with only a few minor complications) they had taken the whole eye out and replaced it with a glass sphere. Oliver couldn't afford the painted porcelain eye that would have made him look almost normal, so he insisted he didn't want it. He said he would paint his own false eyes, on leather patches. And later, he did just that.

After the accident, I was fawned over by everyone as if I had been the one who had lost an eye. I was Oliver's roommate after all, the first to arrive at his side and take his head in my arms. The silent oath I had made to protect his peculiar innocence when I first met him had gone into action immediately. I gave sudden and efficient orders to call 911. And later, of course, there were those times, in the infirmary, when I tried to comfort him as best I could. I remember sitting beside him in a blue metal folding chair fumbling for words that would not come.

"Oli, I'm sorry, really sorry about…well, all this."

"Philip," he said, "don't worry so much. It wasn't your fault. Things happen for a reason, you know that better than anyone right?"

"Sure," I would say. But I didn't really agree. I didn't believe in fate, or destiny or that accidents had any meaning other than the very silver you laid into them yourself. And I for one had long ago given up on that work.

Once, I tried to tell him the truth about it all. But he didn't want to talk about it. He said he didn't really care how it happened or who it was who injured him. He said he wanted nothing to do with blame. He wanted stories instead. So I told him about my summers in Vermont working on my uncle's heavy horse farm, about walking into a narrow stall next to a nervous 1800-pound gelding to dump a bucket of feed. And about the half-ton pile of carrots I had to pick up and deliver once a week. He loved the colors, the scenes, anything that he could see clearly in his head.

Silva, Oliver's stepsister, was often with us, sitting on the other side of the bed rubbing Oliver's back. One night she told him how she thought it had all happened despite his lack of interest. She had been in the pottery studio mixing clay when it happened, but she thought she knew all about it anyway. When Oliver said it was his own fault for not paying attention Silva grew fierce and me along with her.

"That's not true Oli," she said while squeezing the metal sidebars on his bed. "It was some idiot not looking where he was throwing."

I agreed with her completely, of course, and I really did. But then, in his unattached and compassionate way, Oliver defended the unknown idiot aggressor. He would say crazy things like, "Silva, it's not that simple. Sometimes there are unknowable reasons why things happen."

Silva simply wasn't satisfied, in fact she told me later in private that she was tired with her step-brother's enigmatic, mystical bullshit. She wanted justice and a part of me liked her for it.

Despite Oliver's delusions of meaning, or perhaps because of them, I would, late at night, sneak out of the dorm to visit him in the infirmary. We would play cards on the floor next to his bed, or build mythical creatures out of the play-doh I bought for him at the Westfall toy store. Years later, I would look back on those nights as somehow magical and innocent in a simple way. It was as if his wounding allowed me to enter his world deeper than ever before, and in some profound way, to become a part of it.

Yet, despite my connection to Oliver, all during the time he was in the infirmary and forever afterwards, Oliver was the director of our activities together. Even on those nights when Silva was there with me, Oliver was still the one who subtly and gracefully took charge and even gave our consoling a direction and form. He would keep us together talking and eventually turn us inward toward the secret of our hearts. We were each something very special, he would say, as if he knew the truth about us, a truth of which we were at best only dimly aware.

We would sit on the floor while he lay in bed on his stomach and insisted it was true, about how inside each of us there lay something simple and perfect that would carry us through our lives and never abandon us. One night, he told us how he knew this to be true. He said that after he was hit and he fell to the grass he had traveled to a place inside himself, a place behind his mind, and he had learned things, simple things about what and who we really are and will someday be again. Silva and I laughed at his imagination, his dreams of our "divine essence" as he called it. But we desperately wanted to believe him, and wanted to know and see things as Oliver did. But without Oliver there to help us it was impossible, and in the end, perhaps because of this, Silva fell into wanting prophecies. She wanted the good with the bad, as proof of the genuine article. She wanted facts and fortune telling. She pushed him to reveal the truth of her future. But he said he knew nothing about all this, about our failures and successes and the fears and ambitions that would give birth to them. He said he knew only that we were already perfect and nothing could ever change that or add to it."

"There must be something else," she said. "There is always the bad. You know it's true Oli, we have lived it together. Someone must win and someone must lose," she said.

"Difficult times, yes, but no true failures Silva, that I know for sure."

"Then it's only fair to warn us about the difficult times," Silva said and draped her long curly dark hair over his face forming a sanctuary of sorts.

"Just whisper them to me. I promise I won't tell Philip," she said so I could hear her. But Oliver said again that he didn't know about the bad, that he had seen nothing of the darker things, only the truth he said. He had seen only the truth.

## THE ART OF CONFESSION

∆ ∆ ∆

  The enormous pillars were made of brown bricks still waiting to be dressed in marble. Oliver explained to me how centuries ago a Pope had put a stop to the completion of the cathedral because it was designed to be larger than St. Peter's. But the space was still beautiful, despite its unfinished condition, almost more so with its rustic red-brown coloring. There was no one else in this vast house of brick and glass but Oliver, myself, and a few marble saints. It was a good place to get reacquainted.
  I had left for Italy the day before and I was back in his life and he in mine. It was almost like we had never been apart, as if he had never disappeared and three years had not passed since I had last seen him. Of course he was still blind in his left eye. That was never going to change.
  We walked around looking at the frescoes and catching up on the last few years. The floor was a mosaic of small polished red and white stones, and among these were occasional slabs of marble that created designs of stars, planets and dates, all an assortment of messages a twelfth century medieval mind would have been quick

to recognize. There were names of martyred Saints too, and an area where the sun traced the polished rocks revealing all the Catholic holy days in the year. After we had walked for a while and I had told him about my time in college and the friends I had made there, he said to me.

"Philip, I have something I must tell you. It's about Silva." He paused as if wondering whether to go on.

"What is it?"

"You know how she has been looking for her father all these years?

"Yes."

"She thinks he is in Spain and she wants to try and track him down. At least that is what she says."

"She's serious this time?"

"I'm not so sure," he said and turned to face a particularly elaborate stained glass window. "She always drags me into her plans you know?"

"Why don't you just let her find him on her own?"

"I would love to. But right now she needs me to help her pull the money together," he said fishing in his pocket for something. He pulled out a small black triangular item no larger than a quarter.

"You see this," he said holding it out like a gem, "it's a shark tooth. Some sharks swim one stretch of beach their whole lives."

He closed his fist around it and we walked on.

"You know how I have always helped her, Philip. Ever since she was seven years old and she came into my life. She is the only family I care to have know me any more. She has no one else either. My father won't even talk to me for encouraging her to uncover the story about her real father. My stepmother still holds the standard line and says her father is dead. What's worse everyone here in Italy told her the same when she came over, and now the truth is out."

"What can I do?" I asked.

"Keep her busy for me. I am painting right now. I have some work to finish for a show in Milan next month. If I sell some paintings I will give her the money and she can go look for him, like you say, on her own."

We stopped walking to take a look at the shark tooth again. Oliver held his hand out into a beam of light coming through the stained glass. The little black triangle shone like dark sea-glass.

"They lose their teeth all the time. Eventually they wash up on the beach smooth and polished by the waves," he said.

"Sea-teeth."

"Exactly."

He handed it to me and I turned it around several times looking at it in the light.

"I was saving it for you. It's a gift," he said.

"I can't," I said.

"Keep it, please."

It was a genuine animal-charm. I imagined it to be very old and from a large shark. Oliver said finding one this large was rare, which was why he had kept it for me. It was smooth and pointed, black as soot, and shone with a stark fearlessness. I kept it.

spread out wide like wings. A little silence, then back to the candelabrum to secure his wishes. When he was done he put some coins in the small iron strong box. They made a loud metallic tinkling noise as they settled in. The sound spread through the church like metallurgic sin.

"They should line those boxes with felt or something," I said.

Oliver looked at me surprised. "You know, I was thinking the same thing."

"Too bad they don't have a suggestion box," I said.

Oliver had his extra candle in his hand. He extended it toward me.

"Here, I thought you might want to light one. I paid extra," he said with a smile.

This wasn't my custom. In fact, I had none to speak of for this sort of thing, but I took the candle anyway and then made my way up to the candelabra.

It came to me spontaneously, a prayer I think, or perhaps more of a wish. I saw Oliver on the ground the day he lost his eye, crumpled up like a fallen bird. Then, I felt it all again, the instant and overpowering need to help him, to back up time and push him out of the way like Superman, before he got hit. I had wished it, prayed this way, secretly, many times before, for impossible things. I lit the candle, and placed it in the iron holder. Then I walked away somewhat ashamed of my hopeless prayer.

Outside, Oliver was on the steps smoking a clove cigarette. I sat down next to him without a word and enjoyed the fine smell. He offered me the smoke and I took an unfamiliar drag, holding back the cough. The piazza was bustling. People were rushing to the bank or the market perhaps, before the afternoon siesta.

"So how do you paint with all this activity?"

He paused, took back his cigarette. "At dawn it's quiet. There's something especially fine about the morning light here."

He paused to take a long drag.

"Silva and I have been going out to the country on the weekends. To get away from the noise."

"Where do you go?"

"To Angela's, Silva's grandmother. She's got Silva set up with her own kiln. It turns out that the pottery business shut down years ago but they still had all this old equipment so Angela made a deal. If Silva went to the University, then she could have a place in the city and on the weekends she could use the old kilns and studio at the villa."

"Sounds like a great deal."

"I thought so, and it has been for three years. Then Silva went snooping around in places she's not welcome and found some old letters from her father. He is alive. Now she can't wait to leave. She says they lied to her."

"Did they?"

"I think he's dead in their eyes. No one has heard from him in ten years and he left under bad circumstances as you know."

"Right, the Africa thing."

"Yep."

I thought about Silva and how even back in school at Westfall, finding her real father had always been her goal. She had refused to believe that he was dead as her mother had tried to convince her. I had encouraged her in her dream for my own reasons. If there was even a chance he was alive, it seemed worth finding out the truth.

"What about this Angela?" I said, wondering if Silva had ruined another place for herself the way she had ruined Westfall for all of us.

"You'll have to see for yourself. I like her, but she and Silva, well you know how Silva can be, especially now that she is convinced everyone betrayed her. No one is making her leave but I think she will create an exit for herself eventually." He turned to me and his eye crinkled a little to match his rueful smile.

We finished the clove while we sat for a while and watched the pigeons, the people, the ocher walls and stone streets. Everything was alive in the afternoon sun.

We walked back to the bar at the edge of the square, where I had met up with Oliver earlier after my train ride down to Bologna from Milan. My bag was still safely inside by the counter where I left it.

"I have to get back to my job at the museum in a few minutes. I'm helping restore some statuary. Let's meet back here around six," Oliver said.

"What should I do until then?"

"Why don't you go see Silva? She's down the street at the convent. She rents a room there and does some gardening for the nuns."

I asked him if she's still mad at me for what I said to her at the party all those years ago. He said no. She was looking forward to seeing me, to us all being together. "She said she wants you to come over right away," he said. "No doubt, she has some role for you in her escape plan."

Oliver found a well-dressed young man about my age named Antonio in the bar who volunteered to help me find my way to the convent. He had that dark, well-oiled look of the attractive Italian male. Oliver introduced us. He didn't appear to speak much English and he shook my hand a little bit too hard. I wondered if it was the custom.

Oliver sent us both off in the direction of the convent with a gentle one-handed push on my back. I started off and then turned to watch as he walked across the square, turning his head in steady smooth half circles like an owl, to see the whole street. He disappeared into an ancient looking building with massive walls like a castle.

The convent was supposedly two short blocks away on the other side of the cathedral. Antonio looked and smiled at me a few times as we walked but didn't say a word. Something about him made me decide I didn't like him at all. Perhaps it was how very different he made me look. His dark almost coal black hair was slicked back into perfectly coordinated waves and my travel distressed brown hair seemed less than satisfactory. He was shorter by at least a hand, but more muscular than I was. He made me feel like a stork the way he walked calmly ahead of me smoking his cigarette like he owned the world.

When we rounded the first corner of the cathedral he stopped. Then he took out a pack of Marlboros and offered me one. I shook my head. He threw his almost spent one away, lit another up and began to smoke there on the corner, like we were waiting for a bus. I put down my bag and looked around. The street was made of large smooth paving stones and the buildings were covered in some kind of stucco and painted various pale orange, yellow, and red colors. I looked up at the rows of arched windows filled with dark glass, and overhead, in the distance I could see the tops of two enormous towers, the shorter of the two was leaning towards the other as if whispering rumors caught floating up from the web of streets below.

  Then Antonio spoke to me, in Italian. I turned to face him. He said the same thing again, in a vicious tone, like a mean person scolding a dog. I wasn't at all pleased so I spoke back to him quite calmly.

  "You're a bastard," I said.

  He turned and proceeded to walk away waving his hand in the air and talking now to himself. I yelled, "convent" after him.

  He turned, looked at me, as if sizing me up and then pointed down the opposite direction from where he was going. I left and I found the convent a block away. At least he hadn't lied. I hoped it wasn't a friend of Oliver's but just some guy he asked to show me the way who happened to dislike Americans.

  The small triangle of shark tooth poked my leg as I approached the convent doorway. I put down my bag. Then I sat down on the threshold to rest before I saw Silva. I thought about Oliver and how he loved Silva despite her intense need for him. It made me think about the first time I met him and how I had pledged my own loyalty to him, almost at once, and so began my own subtle obsession with his presence.

∆ ∆ ∆

    This is how I remember Oliver and perhaps how my obsession began. He was a tall, thin creature, with a long slow stride. His hands and feet were of the largest variety, the sort, which require a special knowledge of grace to operate without appearing awkward and unseemly. He moved down hills like a stream, on the path of least resistance, and he climbed them slow as summer nights, never in a hurry. I am convinced his pace through life allowed him at least two or three years for every one of my own.

    In our school days we called him Oli, and not Oliver as people call him today. He is famous now, the last paintings he made having sold for a fortune. But when I first met him at Westfall it was a smaller world. Westfall Academy was a private New England school tucked along side the Westfall River. There was a boathouse, a few canoes, a renovated Victorian school building and two old colonial houses for dorms. It was classic New England. Mostly, the students came from towns around Boston and stayed for the day, but Oliver and I lived together in the boys' dorm that sat along Main Street Westfall. I could watch headlights paint their way across my ceiling at night and see the snow fall through the flood light over my window in the winter. Oliver, a painter, was one of our only two foreign students, his step-sister, Silva, who was exceptionally accomplished with the concert harp, was the other. They were both artists, and from Italy or Britain depending on which one you asked. They arrived in the autumn of my senior year, it was September 1987.

I liked Oliver immediately, for what became clear upon his arrival was that he was beyond repair as far as the school was concerned. He didn't register for classes, didn't meet the dean as was prescribed in the handbook, and would not sleep in a proper bed. Silva, who very early became my source of information on my new roommate, said Oliver was special material. She used to come over from the girl's dorm to check on him. She warned me, in her soft, secretive voice, that "Oli doesn't care if anyone likes him." Therefore, I was to look out for him, for "He never looks out for himself." She was right, it would turn out, about many things.

All Oliver brought from London with him was a white canvas bag. In it were a myriad of painting. He walked into the dorm room the first day and over to the closet, looked in, and tossed his bag inside. I was lying there, in my boxers, reading. I was not expecting him for a few hours more.

"This is my room then, right?" he said, pointing to the closet.

My sports coat and slacks were carefully laid over the desk chair. I don't like being surprised, and was about to say so when he turned directly towards me not seeming to take notice of my half-naked state. When I first looked into his eyes it felt like he simply grabbed me with his attention. I was stunned into silence.

He was taller than I was then, of course, but most people at Westfall were in those days. My real growth came on late. He was dressed in an elegant yet baggy assortment of linens: vest, shirt, sports coat, slacks, canvas sneakers, his long fingers and hands half submerged in the frayed cuffs of his shirt and coat. But none of this could really explain it, my silence that is. It was just his presence, it seemed large, larger than anyone I had known in years.

"Sure," I said, about the closet after a long pause.

"Good," he said with vigor.

In that moment of my silence I knew I had somehow lost irretrievable ground and was determined to get it back.

I dressed quickly and then went down to fetch the rest of his bags without asking. I had to return empty handed.

"Where did you go? I thought you'd abandoned me," he said.

"I was just down stairs looking for your bags. There's a girl down there waiting for you to take her to lunch. She said you already have your bag. I thought she was wrong. I mean you only have that one."

"That was Silva, my sister."

"Really, you don't look anything alike."

"Oh, were not blood I just call her that for convenience. It makes my life easier since we go everywhere together. We came together when she was seven and I was eight, step-sister really. And by the way, you should know, Silva is never wrong," he said chuckling and rolling his eyes. "But I do travel light. And you can call me Oli. You are Philip, right?"

How did you know?

"They told me all about you. A real student they said. Just the thing I need. So you can help me with the school stuff, right?"

"Sure," I said, "anything."

We both stood there for a moment. He, looking me over.

"Anything?"

"Well, yeah, if it doesn't break any school rules. I mean I'm not going to cheat for you."

He laughed at that.

"Well then, in that case, can you take Silva to lunch for me. She's driving me mad. I just spent too many hours on a plane with her."

I agreed. I would have agreed to most anything he could have asked of me then, and perhaps that was the problem, maybe he knew.

"And could you pick me up some eggs while you're out," he said. He handed me his canvas bag after carefully emptying the last of its contents out onto the closet floor.

"What sort of eggs? Hard boiled?"

"No, just the regular sort."

"We don't have a kitchen here in the dorm."

He looked at me for a moment as if I had spoken in a foreign language.

"I see. Right...well....then, could you get them for me anyway?"

His look held me there. This is the test, I thought. He didn't waste any time. He wanted to know where I stood, loyal roommate, or coward.

"Okay, I'll get a carton for you."

"Really?" he said and touched my shoulder, genuinely thankful.

"Sure, I can do it. Everyone works in the kitchen here. I know where they are."

"Right then, good luck," he said in his English way, as if I were his very own child heading out on an Easter egg hunt. I decided this was some European thing, like kissing on both cheeks. But I was fooling myself. From that moment forward my life would never be quite the same. Oliver had entered the picture and instantly found me lacking. I was sure if it. I was not five-seconds gone from him before I set out to prove him wrong.

∆ ∆ ∆

I sat on the threshold of the convent thinking for some time before I was ready to see Silva again. I finally knocked on the door and she came down to get me after the little old nun in black who answered the door disappeared for ten minutes. It wasn't awkward like I thought it would be. Her hair was longer and fuller than I remembered. When she saw me we hugged and her arms were strong like a potter's should be. She was the same height as she was back in Westfall and I taller.

"Philip, you've grown up and up," she said while clutching my hands in hers and her eyes alight. She pulled me in the convent door by the sleeve and then took me up to her apartment. She made me feel at home: tea, the washroom, some bread and cheese were in order. She was delighted to see me. She commented on the wire-rimmed glasses that I had acquired since I had seen her last. It had been three years, same as with Oliver. She said I looked sophisticated and I felt that way with her there telling me it was so, as if anything she said was true just because it came from her. After some time drinking tea by the window and looking down at the deserted alley and talking old times, she had to leave. I was tired, so she left me alone for a few hours while she went out to shop for dinner. I tried to sleep, and I did for a couple of hours, but my dream was full of a dark frozen river with men chopping holes in the ice in search of something they had lost. I woke up still tired and unwilling to think about the dream. Instead I explored the interior of the convent. I found a small chapel and rested there in front of the statue of the Virgin and child and watched the light cross their bodies and then leave them in shadow as the sun set.

Later that night Oliver, Silva and myself made some food in her apartment. We had fettuccine, with salami and mushrooms, bread and olive oil. We drank some red table wine and sat in front of the warm fireplace. The candles Silva lit completed the medieval feel of the place with its stone floor and oak beams. The four corners of the room were draped in soft darkness and the stark wooden convent furniture wedded itself to the shadows well. It all would have felt perfect if I could have stopped myself from wondering if Silva might still be angry with me for my less than cordial behavior at my graduation party years ago. That was the last time I had seen her and I was convinced at the time that she had betrayed me. Maybe she had, I still didn't know. But on some level it didn't seem to matter anymore.

Silva and I sat in front of the fire on the large throw rug, limbs heavy and lazy with the table wine. Silva smiled and laughed a lot at small things, like my glasses, which were a great novelty for some reason. She was like that when she drank; the hard edge melted off her and a wonderful felicity grew from within and spread out into the room. I gathered it up, what I could of it, and drank at the sweetness of her smile which always evoked in me a not unpleasant mix of desire and ease. Always, it seemed the possibility of a future clandestine moment between us lingered at the fine edges of her eyes.

Oliver on the other hand grew somber. He was laying on his side behind us on the edge of the bed. He had his sketchbook open and was working on something. It was good to see him drawing. It appeared to ease his seeming flight into gloomy looking thoughts.

I poked at the fire. The large log was sitting squat on a bed of coals. It didn't budge when I poked it and so I played with the coals around the edges to keep things lively. Oliver rolled off the bed and stood up. He went to the door where the wood was stacked and brought some smaller scraps of kindling over and dropped them around the edges of the fire.

"Should we go out tomorrow?" he said.

"We can take the car into the country," Silva said. She got up and poured herself another glass of wine and then sat down again.

"We don't have to go anywhere right away," I said.

"No, we should go somewhere," Oliver said.

"Yes," agreed Silva with a laugh. "We should go somewhere."

We sat quietly around the fire for some time then looking at the flames and chatting about the best of our old days at Westfall.

Later that night, after Oliver had gone to his studio elsewhere in the city, Silva said, "I am glad you came. Oliver really needs an old friend right now."

"Why?"

"To take care of me while he paints, so he says. But I think he has something he wants to tell you."

"What?"

"I can't tell you, but I am sure he will get around to it." Then she kissed me on the cheek and retired to her room. I stayed up and looked out the convent window at the alley below. A small cat was sitting in the middle of the street.

It seemed to me that they both needed a little space from each other. I was open to helping, yet, as the thought passed through my mind, I felt an old uneasiness. I had learned, years ago, that things were never exactly as they appeared to be between them. The idea that Oliver had something to reveal to me was unsettling. Oliver had a way of getting inside a person and upsetting things that are better left alone. It began to rain and the cat walked away to find a better place to sit and be. I got up and made my way to the couch where I was sleeping and remembered my early days with both of them back in Westfall, before the trouble began. I spent several hours thinking things over before I finally fell asleep.

Δ   Δ   Δ

On the day Oliver arrived at Westfall Academy, I took Silva to lunch like he asked me. I used what little social capital I had accumulated that year as I sat down next to Teresa Agarr. I said something like, *Teresa, this is Silva. She's European.* That was all I needed to do. Silva was easy to deliver; she was outgoing and attractive, with curly Italian hair and thin hips. I took her to the table where all the popular attractive girls sat, figuring to start Silva at the top. I wasn't true friends with these girls, but I knew them all by name because of Teresa, the prettiest of them all, with whom I shared an academic locker space in the Jefferson Building.

Teresa was feeling generous that day. She gave me her sweetest smile after the introduction and to my surprise took right over from there. I was allowed to sink into the silence I preferred. I ate my buttered carrots and mashed potatoes and watched the subtle weave of attractive popular girls carefully crafting a new alliance.

Later, I left Silva with Teresa and prowled my way into the kitchen, and then over to the walk-in refrigerator. For the first time in my life I acted, felt like and indeed was a thief. What was I doing stealing eggs for a roommate I didn't even know? I asked myself, as I searched for a full carton. I put the carton carefully into the canvas bag Oliver had loaned me walked back to the dorm. I thought I made it back undiscovered but within two days Oliver received a note to visit his advisor Mr. Dylan, ostensibly to see how Oliver was settling in. But I was worried the stolen eggs had been discovered by someone in the dorm and reported. To my disbelief Oliver didn't attend the meeting, instead he simply wrote back on the card that he felt very much like a chameleon on the move, which was the school mascot, and thanks for the concern. Then, a week later, after his first face to face encounter with Mr. Dylan, Oliver returned with the word RESPOND written in bold blue letters across his forehead.

"Look what they have done to me," he wailed in mock suffering. "This is my scarlet letter," he said. "They say I must wear it until I am reformed. You Americans are pitiless."

"They know about the eggs then?"

"Of course they do, everyone saw you...."

"How, Oli? No one...."

Oliver took the blame for me. Somehow he had convinced them that I was not at fault, that he had set the whole thing up and I bore no responsibility. How they knew eggs were even missing is beyond me. I thought I had been clever and stealthy.

Oliver wasn't listening to me as I protested him taking all the blame. He went on talking about how they had held him down on a large oak table and drawn the tortuous letters of the word RESPOND with heavy-handed strokes. I didn't believe him and said so. He was stunned for a moment and then he admitted he had done it himself in the bathroom after the interrogation. I was impressed he could write so legibly backwards in a mirror and told him. He shrugged it off. The letters were spread evenly and smoothly in blue ink across his pale, almost sallow skin. It took a few days before it wore off. But while it lasted it drew attention to him around campus, and perhaps me as well, for I was almost always by his side whenever possible. We were the egg thieves, and students and teachers alike quickly came to think of us as a unit: Oli and Philip. I gained some notoriety from the association, for everyone at school quickly knew of Oliver--his smooth, elongated gait, the pale blond hair and eyebrows, small ears, thin lips, and his one extraordinary feature, his deep carnelian-brown eyes. Other than the intense gaze, his features were delicate. At times, when one saw him, he looked to be a girl or a boy or some mix of both. Most odd, when one was very close, I mean truly near, his eyes became as soft as an old dog–large with love.

But Oliver and his features were of a quiet sort and did not respond, it seemed, to anything I did. That was the core of his problem. He told me himself. He had not been responding correctly all his life.

"I must learn to get to class on time they tell me, eat lunch at noon, dinner in the evening, sleep at night, awake at dawn, and stop stealing eggs.

"Oli, I stole the eggs. Why did they call you in?"

He ignored my question as we headed out of the dorm.

"Philip, what will become of me!" He sparkled with amusement at his absurd sufferings and at the cool autumn air, kicking the leaves as he went. We were on our way to the library, walking under the enormous oak trees.

"There must be another way to interpret this word RESPOND," he said, "either that or I will end up turning myself inside out in order to fit into this world of yours Philip."

In the library we stood in front of a massive dictionary printed in miniature type. A few students I regularly saw in the library were looking at him, then me, with curiosity. Oliver was not being particularly quiet. With an authoritative flourish he brought out the magnifying glass he always carried in his pocket, and he said "RESPOND" loud and clear. "TO ANSWER, TO REPLY, TO HAVE A POSITIVE OR FAVORABLE REACTION, TO BE LIABLE."

"Lord!" he said, raising his head, "I am definitely not liable! I will not have anyone lying on top of me."

I had to lean over and peer through the smooth rounded glass to read it myself. Oliver held it steady for me.

Oliver looked at me, puzzled.

"What?" I said.

"You're awfully slow," he said.

"But I get it all. I read the whole thing. You didn't. You didn't understand it. It has nothing to do with sleeping."

"Yes I did, and who said anything about sleep?"

I was about to take issue with him when he raised the glass to his eye, brought his face close to mine. He was standing too close. Oliver looked at me, long and hard, without moving or blinking, without even breathing it seemed.

"Stay still, Philip. How am I supposed to check your eyes?"

I couldn't move. Everyone in the library was watching us. I could feel their eyes trying to look through that damn glass along with Oliver to see what was wrong with me.

"Just as I suspected."

"What?" I said.

"Your eyes are in perfect condition."

The librarian took notice. Mr. Storkerson's library had been a second home for me before Oliver arrived. Since then I had been noticeably absent. It was just one of the many stable patterns I had created over the first three years of high-school that began to shift under Oliver's influence.

I stepped away from Oliver and gave a shaky wave at Mr. Storkerson while Oliver calmly put his glass away. Storkerson frowned at me and went into the back room. Oliver looked smugly at me.

"So?" I said.

"Isn't it obvious?" he said, turning back to the dictionary.

"Isn't what obvious?"

He flipped some pages and then closed the book. "You don't know how to use your own eyes properly."

I was stunned at the insult. I held back what was going to be a retort of some weight and wit because Oliver had picked up the dictionary in his arms like it was a lost child and was walking away with it.

"Let's go," he said over his shoulder.

"What?"

"Are you deaf also? Let's go!"

As we left I realized that Oliver didn't play fair. It was weeks before I came to see what I had missed that day: Oliver possessed a photographic memory. He needed only one glance and he had it all, forever carved into the marble of his mind. I understood suddenly why school was never a concern for him. He never seemed to study; he just flipped through the books once during the first week and then left them stacked on the floor. It was impossible for him to be liable for his actions, he said. He was bored by everything they tried to teach him. He had already read all the books they had to give him, had seen all the paintings, the math problems, and essay questions elsewhere.

Despite his encyclopedic mind, I believed that most of all, Oliver just didn't care what the school, or anyone, thought of him, just as Silva had said. I wasn't even sure what he was doing in school.

"I'm painting, Philip," he said, when I asked him.

"It's as good a place as any. Don't you think?"

For a while I thought he just needed time to adjust, but he never did. He wouldn't follow a schedule of any sort but his own. Silva finally explained it to me. Oliver, she said, lives in a twenty-six-hour day. This was the only way he could labor for his art, outside the normal scope of time, she said. Practically speaking, it meant he might actually get somewhere on time only once a month, and that his sleeping patterns and eating habits were at odds with not only the school, but the sun, the moon, the planet itself.

I suspected that Oliver was perhaps the deeply angry sort, holding a silent grudge against the powers that be. But it wasn't so. He had no qualm with the administration or the solar system, or any other authority figure. I could divine no cherished slight, half-forgotten or otherwise, responsible for his bizarre behavior. He was simply unconcerned with what was correct and proper, and to my chagrin, he was one of those mysterious people who, for some unfathomable reason, was capable of getting away with it.

When we returned to the safety of our dorm room that day, we continued reading the dictionary. The trip across campus from the library with the large book had been a nervous one for me. It was high noon and Oliver chatted with whomever we met along the way. He was particularly congenial to the head mistress, but not once did anyone take notice or discuss the tome that Oliver rested on his shoulder.

"You see, Philip, there is a difference between seeing and looking. Almost anyone can look, but very few actually see what is right in front of them," he said and joggled the dictionary in his arms for emphasis.

We laid the book out on the bureau and opened to the R section again: RESPONDER, RESPONDENT, RESPONSIBLE, RESUSCITATE. Oliver was quite taken by RESUSCITATE. "TO RAISE UP," he said, "TO REVIVE."

Oliver knew instinctively that the book would add importance to our room. When we, or anyone we trusted, was at a loss for words, they would know whom to come to.

"We have begun a life of literate crime, my friend," he said.

∆  ∆  ∆

The next morning Oliver woke me up when he opened the heavy oak door of the convent room with a bang.

"Come on Philip, let's show you the world."

It was early when Oliver came, pre-dawn. He insisted on the hour, saying that he wanted me to witness Piazza Grande as the sun rose. A low-lying September mist was lingering about our ankles as we walked. The stone paved streets looked as if they had exhaled a ghost.

Oliver and I stopped at the same bar where we had met the day before. We left with a bag of warm pastries in hand and ate them as we walked across the square. The marble steps of the Cathedral spanned one entire side of the massive piazza while what appeared to be old administration buildings filled out the other three sides.

Oliver was fiddling with his eye-patch as we went. It bothered me sometimes to see him adjusting it in public. Other times I was proud of him for not being ashamed. He never seemed to notice when someone stared at him.

"I'm used to it," he told me once.

As we left the piazza, the moment arrived when the city was beautiful in its waking, slow, calm, and serene. The perfect time to paint. We entered the massive portal of a building near the piazza and took an old elevator to the rooftop where a little brick roof-house stood arrayed with at least a dozen tall narrow windows along three of its four walls. It looked like it may have been used as some kind of greenhouse before it was converted into a studio. Somehow, Silva had managed to find Oliver one of the highest spots in the city for his studio; most of the buildings weren't very tall in the old city, so it was an impressive achievement. I could see the sprawl of new buildings out beyond the medieval walls and then far off a haze that must have been the city turning into fields. We walked up a set of stairs along the one windowless side of the studio up to a flat roof where a few chairs were set up.

"At night, I can see the lights on the hills," Oliver said. He stood and looked out for a moment and then sat down in one of the chairs. Not far from us were the two medieval city towers I had seen the day before from below. Oliver said that from on top of the tallest, on a clear night, the lights of Milan could be seen. I sat down, and together we finished the pastries Oliver had bought at the bar. I looked out at the dawn. The red tiled roofs, which spread out like a field below us, melted into one massive village of jumbled faces. Many of the scattered roofs had pools or sun decks marking the secret world of sun worship.

Oliver pulled out a cigarette and played with it. He rolled it up and down the arm of his chair with his long fingers. I noticed again that his hands looked older than the rest of him, the skin more stretched. I knew it was probably from all the paint he used, but it still didn't look good.

"So why did you really come here, Philip?" he said.

I looked away from him. He had always been this way, going quickly to the heart of things. He put his left hand out and placed it on mine for a moment.

"Because you asked me to," I said. "You sent that postcard."

"I sent you dozens of cards over the last three years."

I didn't say anything, but when he took his hand back I felt myself relax. He turned to let his face capture the sun coming up over the city. Then he brought out his magnifying glass and handed it to me. I saw the crack in it.

"How?"

"In a secluded park by a statue of Venus. I refused a woman who wanted to make love. She threw my glass and it hit Venus's left breast and the glass cracked. She was mad. Never deny a woman Philip, unless you absolutely have to."

"So why did you?"

"I was feeling sick. She didn't want to hear it. She got angry as you can imagine."

knowing that he was human after all. That indeed suffering had actually registered upon the path of his life and altered his course.

As I lay there on the cold bricks, I started slowly drifting through my memories of him, back to our earliest days together at Westfall. I am not sure what I was looking for, perhaps some hint as to what went wrong and why. I remembered how our dorm room closet became Oliver's studio and in a sense, his home. It was large as far as closets go, a small room actually, ten feet wide, eight deep, eight to touch the ceiling and with its own small circular window that opened and thus allowed him to get way with smoking. He slept in that closet on the very first night he arrived, pulling the mattress off the metal bed frame by the window and folding it in half to get it though the closet door. Then he carefully placed his dozen eggs in the corner where he was sure not to step or roll on them in the night.

"Oli, what are you going to do with those eggs?" I asked.

"Waiting for them to hatch," he said as he shut the closet door and closed me out. I listened for the revolting sound of raw eggs being eaten but it didn't happen. His closet, I learned in the first weeks, was where he labored, waited, and struggled to paint. He murmured and fought with himself in there, measured, weighed and mixed his precious colors like an alchemist, smoked his clove cigarettes, and had private conversations with his creations. After he moved himself in I stayed away from the closet for some time. I wasn't going to tell anyone he was smoking cloves but I wasn't going to be near it either. In the first three years of high school I had developed allergies, and from them a mild case of asthma. I didn't need the smoke despite that I loved the smell of the cloves.

With Oliver in the closet, I kept my clothes in piles around my bed. I would never have used the hangers much anyway since my belongings tended to become disordered over the semester. Oliver on the other hand possessed a disordered look that hid a subtle and economic organization that I attributed to some English tradition I lacked. He kept all his belongings inside his closet with him, objects mostly, things he collected that had caught his eye and could be transformed and combined to create something new. He had that bronze Buddha of course that he had found on a curb set out for the garbage one day, a broken antique wooden cradle he kept for his painting supplies, a red floppy hat from the thrift shop, a triple beam balance from the science lab, a step ladder, and of course the massive dictionary he used as a simple night stand for his blue tin mug. As a door stop he had a motel size copy of the Bible, which was perpetually scraping back and forth over the old wooden floor as he adjusted the door for the light appropriate for an afternoon of painting.

Sometime in late September, several weeks after school had begun, I was standing at the threshold of the closet engulfed in the intoxicating aromas of oil paints and cloves, waiting, but hesitant to pass into his domain. I had never been into the closet once it became his. At least, not while he was around. It was his space.

I peered into the inky dark. Oliver looked up at me, his face spotted with a few blue and red finger dashes of the oils he used. He took a long drag off his cigarette and held me there, in his gaze while he let it out slowly.

In those early weeks, before we became true friends, I had tried to earn Oliver's respect through some intellectual discourse. I was convinced I had mostly failed. But I was still trying to nail him down and get him to see some things my way on subjects like loyalty for instance. We were, after all, to be roommates for a year, and loyalty was the only thing one could really depend on. He said he wasn't so sure.

"Friends are human," he said, "and everything human breaks, especially love."

"What good is a belief like that?" I said.

"It's not a belief Philip, it's a fact."

He took another long drag off his cigarette and then he held up something in his hand, covering it with his fingers. I could see colors beneath, and elaborate patters of some kind.

"If you believe in something, you can imbue it with life Philip," he said with a quick smile, "but if you then experience that same something, you no longer need your belief, because it reveals itself to you, so you just know it. And rarely is the belief you imbued the same as the experience you come to know."

He squinted his eyes at me as if looking into the sun and held out his hand as if to give me something.

"Don't look at me like that," I said and just stood there annoyed by all the fumes and my own foolishness for engaging him in conversation such as this. I ignored his outstretched hand for too long and he went back to his painting as if I wasn't standing there.

"Philip, now you're standing in the light."

I persisted in my lingering.

"Philip, either come in or go out, you can't stand there blocking the afternoon. It only comes once a day."

I went in and sat in the corner. There beside me was the carton of eggs. It was closed and I was afraid to open it and see the mess. But there was no stench. So while Oliver was readying his paints I looked in the carton and I found them all in tact but one.

"Oli, what are you doing with these?"

"I am going to paint on them."

I picked one up. It was too light.

"What did you do with the insides?"

"I emptied them out with a needle and fed them all to the cat who lives in the bushes out back."

"That was nice of you."

"Yes...it was."

"Here, have this." He opened his hand and inside it was an egg.

"Take it," he said and held it out for me to inspect. I put out my hands like a cup and he laid it on my palms.

"I made it for you," he said.

I looked up at him incredulous.

"You managed the theft. It was the least I could do."

In that moment, I knew I was looking at one of the most beautiful objects I had ever seen. Covering the shell were interwoven colored lines, ancient and medieval looking designs of the kind I had once seen in pages copied from the Book of Kells. Woven into the minute lacing were the abstracted bodies of people, horses, and fabulous blue winged birds. I looked deep into the minute details and I understood suddenly why Oliver carried a magnifying glass with him. In one small sloping inch of that egg there were hundreds of impossibly minute and perfect connections. No human eye could possible keep up such focus for long without help.

Oliver had asked of me at least a dozen favors since he had arrived. I had lived under his absurd attitude and uncomfortable stare, and all along he had been making this gift for me. What came back to me was a hundred fold what I had given him.

That afternoon I stayed in the closet for a long time despite the smoky atmosphere. He said I could keep the egg. I refused. It had taken him two weeks to create it. I simply could never keep such a thing. He insisted and proceeded to take it from me and then threaded fishing line through it with a needle. We went into my room and he hung it above my pillow from a thumbtack.

"It is one endless golden and green snake, never broken, never fractured, infinite and biting its own tail. It will protect you from your bad dreams," he said.

I looked at him.

"I can hear you at night, Philip. You talk. You aren't happy in there," he said and touched his oil covered finger to my heart.

I looked at his finger and then at the red dot of paint he left on my white oxford when he took it away. Then, with his clean hand he reached up and gave the shell a gentle twist, and we watched, together, as it spun over my pillow.

It was that afternoon that I suddenly began to speak freely to Oliver. No one had ever given me such a gift before, and the act of kindness seemed to open a door between us that connected me to Oliver in a way I was connected to no one else in the world. A door that promised to lead to unknown possibilities and one which I would one day never want to close.

With such promise hanging in the air between us like so much gold to be mined I began to tell him stories about my dreams. My dreams were my secret inner life and always had been. Without them it seemed like life would have been intolerable. I had the full range of dreams from ecstasy to nightmare, but I took the bad with the good because in the end, my dreams were the only loyal friends I had. They always came to me, and they were rich beyond what the outer world had offered me in years.

I told him about a dream I had the night before that contained elements from an old family tragedy that my uncle Bernard told me about years ago. It was a terrible story really, but I told him anyway. It happened in the late thirties in Vermont. My grandfather was driving a team of his best Percherons, pulling some hay, when a rich sportsman, with a fancy car, drove around a bend in the road too fast. It was late afternoon and the sun setting, and so my grandfather thinks the sportsman probably couldn't see a thing when he rounded the corner. The sportsman drove straight under the legs of the horses. The horses and the diver never knew what hit them. They all eventually died, man and horses, all except my grandfather who had to shoot his best team and walk six miles to the next town to tell someone about it.

I went on for some time, about how after it happened my grandfather, my mothers' father, had moved the family horse farm to a small island on Lake Champlain after that, and then never left. He just lived in the past.

Oliver looked amazed.
"That was gruesome, Philip."
"Yes, I have some gruesome dreams."

"No wonder you don't sleep well."
I nodded.
"Does it help to tell them out loud."
"I guess so."

So that was how it began for Oliver and I, our friendship and collaboration. Out of a painted egg, came a dream and the birth of our ritual. From then on, in the pre-dawn when I would awake I would rise with my vivid dreams still swimming in my mind's eye and stumble toward his closet. Each time I entered I found him awake and ready to listen to me while he painted bits and pieces of my secret world onto his walls. Eventually the closet was always adrift in colors and scenes, some were horrible and some beautiful, and all of them revealed a small fragment of the inner world that I carried within me and had never before spoken of to anyone.

In those early weeks of our collaboration, I often felt a loss when a part of my inner world would vanish beneath another newer work. Oliver said each had lived out its purpose, and not to fear, because each would come back in its own time to be remade into something more beautiful. Letting them all go, he said, was as much a part of the process as letting them out.

"Loss is a sacred process," he said. "It is the only way to make room for new life and new beauty." And in time, I became more comfortable with the process, less perhaps because I believed him, and more because Oliver himself had a big and open heart. He was not afraid to grieve right in front of me when he too had to let go of one of the paintings he had particularly loved.

∆ ∆ ∆

I don't know how long I lay on the floor under the many rendered eyes but I arrived back in the present with a jolt. Perhaps some noise had awakened me, I didn't know. But I felt a pleasant affinity for the past. I still have the painted egg Oliver made for me. It is in a glass case at home in Westfall.

I sat up a bit too fast and strained my neck a little as I did so. In a cupboard I found a few mugs and put some water on to boil for tea.

Lying about were small sketched portraits of people I didn't know. They all seemed lean and underfed, as if being consumed from the inside out by some insatiable thirst. Some were half painted over, others were completely covered, hidden by layers of oil. Once again Oliver's aims were mysterious.

On the table I saw a large black sketchbook. I opened it and paged through. There were dozens and dozens of people, sad looking portraits mostly. So many I had to close the book because they all looked so distraught, and all of them naked. Even the children looked like victims of war.

"Hi there!"

I turned around a little to quickly.

Oliver smiled, laughed at my surprise and walked over to check the teapot.

"I hope you don't mind me snooping."

"Snoop away."

The water was boiling on the stove and sending steam up. Oliver put the water to its purpose in the cups, added the tea bags and searched a tiny fridge for some cream and a piece of ice to cool it all down to how he liked it.

"Sugar?"

I didn't say anything and he put it in. He knew I loved pure sugar as much as he did.

He finished with the tea and lit a half-smoked cigarette, which he found on the stove. He handed me my tea.

"Are you covering over all your sketches for a reason?" I said.

He turned around and looked at me and then his work.

"I started doing it with a pencil, two actually, soft and hard leads. I have a whole book full of them to finish off. I have sketches of everyone I met in my travels."

"Why hide them? Are they going to come back better some day like all my old dreams?"

He stood at the window for a moment.

"No, these will never come back. I'm just letting them go. It's a meditation of sorts, on dying."

I waited a long while and I started to wonder if he would say anything more.

"I would like to be able to tell you more about it Philip, the past, but not right now, Okay?"

My right hand was warm from the mug and my left chilled from the morning air and everything around me. Then he walked up behind me and stood close to me as he often did. It made me tense and nervous at first.

Steam was rising from his tea. I felt the warmth against my face and I could feel his body very near. It had always been this way, as if his body extended beyond his physical form, and when he was close I felt as if I was inside him. And in those moments I sometimes felt like I was falling, and other times, as if I had been found.

Δ  Δ  Δ

*My mother and I are sitting on the couch in the family room watching Fred Astaire and Ginger Rogers waltzing around the gray of my father's old black-and-white television. Elise, my mother, is beaming in recognition of the divine movements visible to her trained eye.*

*She once met Fred Astaire in New York City. I shared a cup of coffee with him, she said. She always said this.*

*We are watching the screen. She likes to refer to Mr. Astaire as Fred. She says, "divine, Fred, just divine." There seems to be a secret conversation taking place of which I am only remotely aware. My father is there now. They are dancing, the two of them. I am sitting on the couch and watching them dance through the kitchen, library, dining, and sitting rooms. My parents are Fred and Ginger. I believe this. I create memories of them, of us, in our house, at the dinner table, the club, by the river, and my last memory, when they were leaving, out the front door heading for the West Coast for films, and fame.*

Δ  Δ  Δ

My second morning in Italy was as gray as it was cold. I brushed the hair from my forehead with my hand and looked out the window. I heard Silva and Oliver talking in her bedroom and wondered what it was about. I had a sense it was about me. But it is easy to think things are about oneself.

"What do you mean wait, that it will take care of itself," she said.

"I am not going to force this Silva."

"That wasn't your fault. Don't be ridiculous."

"It will happen on its own if you will just let it," Oliver said.

Then there was silence and Silva came out the door of the bedroom in a green robe and walked to the bathroom. She didn't see that I was awake.

We left for the country later that morning. A light rain was falling from a low heavy sky, and as we climbed into the hills we passed through banks of drifting fog. During the ride Oliver asked if he could paint my portrait. I didn't like the idea. Oliver tended to unravel a person through the portrait process and I wasn't prepared for that. I had things I didn't want him to see in me just yet. Things I wanted to reveal on my own terms. But I also didn't want to disappoint him, so I said it was a definite maybe. I figured I could just "maybe" my way through my entire stay and leave without having to sit for him. I changed the subject by asking Silva questions about her grandmother. Silva said Angela was a lump of coal, a woman made of endless layers of black cloth who carries around an enormous umbrella that she taps on the hard floors as she shuffles around the house like a blind person.

"You will meet Husband too, her donkey. She is never without that animal," Oliver said.

"Husband is a blind albino and wouldn't survive without her," Silva said. I didn't believe her and said so.

"Oh, all the men are blind in our family."

Oliver ignored her.

We were driving along narrow roads through small medieval towns and rolling fields up and up into the hills. Home for Angela was, and had always been, a large vineyard and villa built by a Cardinal in the eleven hundreds. On the way we saw all the common things of the country one sees everywhere in the world, but to me, every old farmhouse was an adventure missed. We even passed a castle. I made Silva turn the car around to investigate, but there were "No Trespassing" signs posted in Italian all along the driveway, or so she said. As we climbed higher into the hills the roads became narrow. I was in the back seat behind Silva, who was driving. I was worried. She was speeding, or at least seemed to be; taking corners at a reckless pace considering the wetness of the roads. She honked regularly so if anyone coming towards us happened to hear in time they could sacrifice themselves and swerve off the road. I looked out my window and down a steep hill that tumbled away rapidly through the scattered fog and clouds. The road below was all snakes. I found it hard to imagine we had actually survived the traversing.

"Silva," I said, "not a lot of traffic on this road?"

"Nope, everyone who leaves goes down hill in the morning, and they don't come up until dinner. It's just too far of a drive to and from the valley with the flooding."

The hills around the villa fell sharply away from each other due to the deep cuts made by retreating glaciers and ages of run off. A vast rolling grid of grapevines spread out over them in blankets of brown and green, and the villa was perched like a nest on the side of one small hill near a village that sat at still a higher altitude. We passed a grassy, tree-scattered field, then turned right at a small church and headed down a cobbled drive with old carriage ruts. Finally, we came to a standstill in a muddy flagstone carport. A family of three, mother, daughter and father were leaving on foot as we pulled in. Silva gave them a wave and said the young woman would be married soon and that the reception was being held at the villa the next weekend.

Above us were towering an enormous row of Italian Cypress trees that just barely swayed in the breeze. Bordering the area was a three-foot stone wall, and beyond that a drop off which fell away to the first level of gardens almost two stories down. I wasn't feeling well as I climbed out of the back seat of the small car. I had done too much looking out the window during the last few miles of our drive up into the hills. The air around us more or less hovered about in a languid and mesmerizing drizzle: Slow, rhythmic, subtle waves of water washed over my cold face. We all stood outside the massive barn sized wooden double doors of the old villa for a moment, our faces held up to the sky with thin veils of soft water falling over us.

"Does it rain like this often?" I asked, with my eyes open to the slate sky above.

"All the time this September it seems," Oliver said.

"It's beautiful," Silva said.

Then a light went on over our heads as a door swung open. An older woman with marble smooth skin stood there glowing with the warm light issuing from within. She was maybe fifty. She wore a white apron and her hands were still covered in flour. She clapped and dusted them on her sides as she took Silva into her arms and then Oliver. This was Carina, Silva's aunt. She stood above us, on a step. I looked up at her and she took me into her arms as well. She smelled of fresh warm bread and vanilla, a fine mix of earth and heaven.

"Come, come, come in. We have been here, waiting, waiting, waiting," she said. "Angela in library and needs you *immediatamento,* Silva. Come in, your coats, here, I have them."

She took our jackets and hung them on a row of hooks along the wall beside the door.

"I send Camillo for your things, he's just sitting around all day like a lazy dog," she said with a charming laugh and then left us in the hall and walked toward what smelled like baking bread.

Silva tuned to me and smiled sweetly. Then she asked Oliver to go tell Angela that we had arrived and that she could meet me, Philip, after I had settled into my room. Oliver swung his canvas bag over his shoulder and adjusted his patch slowly.

"All right. When will you come up?"

"Why don't you tell her we will meet at dinner."

Oliver didn't have to say it. It was clear from his face that he didn't like the idea.

"Well, we could just go meet her now. I mean, I don't feel too sick," I said.

"No, Philip, it's okay, you should rest, she can wait. It won't kill her."

"Okay, I'll tell her you're not well," Oliver said and then quickly turned and walked away through a Roman arch and up some stairs.

"What was that all about?"

"Nothing. Don't worry about it. She just has these rules."

"Well, maybe we should..."

"Nope, it's good for the old raven to have her feathers ruffled every so often."

Silva quickly turned her attention to the hall that surrounded us and gave me no room to argue. The hall was large, a medieval banquet room. She said it was still used regularly, like at the wedding reception that would take place on the next weekend. The double doors leading into the great hall were of enormous barn like dimensions, and a small door set inside one of them had been opened for us to enter. A large stone fireplace sat at the far end of the room. There was some wood stacked nearby but only a low flame was flickering over a bed of coals at the moment. The room was chilled to heavy sweater temperature and the illumination was just above minimal.

"Come, come," Carina said coming back in from the kitchen. "It is warmer in here."

Silva was rubbing her hands together against the cold. As we followed Carina, Silva said she would be doing the decorating and some cooking for the wedding reception. "So I will be a little busy this week."

"Maybe I can help," I volunteered.

"You wouldn't mind?"

"No, I will need something to do."

"But this is your vacation, Philip."

"I like to feel useful."

"Okay then," she conceded with a sweet smile that made me feel a little better than volunteering to assist her should have.

In the kitchen there were three brick ovens baking bread and a pile of wood in the corner. The table I sat at was a large, all-purpose kitchen table in the center of the room. In the corner a Zenith black and white TV was on, and an old episode of *Dallas* flickered uncertainly.

Carina smiled and pointed at *Dallas* with a knife, "America," she said. Then she turned her attention back to the tomatoes she had lined up in front of her, and there was a bowl of fruit on the table as well. She was eating grapes from it every now and then. The show was dubbed in Italian and yet I could tell exactly what was happening regardless. I remembered the episode vaguely. For one season Oliver and I watched the show together back in Westfall at my house when my father was staying at his new apartment on Beacon hill. We would sit in the leather easy chairs and make drinks for ourselves, things we had to teach ourselves to make from a book like: Manhattan, Sloe-Gin-Fizz, Margarita. Often enough Oliver sketched during the show and at the end of the season he had a few good portraits of JR and the other main characters, which he gave to me.

Silva laid out some warm bread, olive oil, tomatoes and mozzarella for me on a plate. Carina made me a cappuccino. The warmth came back into my body and some of the grogginess left as well. Silva and Carina spoke in Italian and I pretended to watch *Dallas* as if I was interested. I saw that Carina and Silva were close. It was good to see Silva this way. I suspected that Carina might be the first person in her family, besides Oliver, that Silva had really opened herself too since her father vanished when she was a child.

Carina's English was not as expert as Silva's Italian was, but she could understand what I said. There was talk of our trip into the hills and then what we would have for dinner. She gave Silva a naughty child look when she explained we had not seen Angela yet.

"Silva, likes difficult," she said to me and smiled. Silva turned a little red in the cheeks. I liked her, this Carina, she seemed to float with ease through what was obviously the same sort of trouble that seemed to follow Silva wherever she went.

In the corner was a cooking fireplace with a large stump burning, which kept us warm enough. After I finished my coffee Silva poured us both a glass of the red wine from the villa's vineyard. She insisted I taste it right away.

"It's part of the tradition here," she said. "You have to try the wine as soon as possible, they are very proud of it, you know. They sell and ship it all over Italy, Europe and the world."

Carina smiled at us both. I wondered if Silva was making some of this up. She was prone to exaggeration or alterations of the truth if they fit the circumstances she had imagined or preferred to see.

We carried our wine with us as Silva took me through the first floor of the villa to the room I would be staying in. It was beautiful, with two large windows looking over the valley below. She told me the view was even better when the clouds were not so low and dreary. Down two steps and through an arch was my own private sitting room with fireplace, overstuffed chairs, and low vaulted ceilings.

"Is this okay for you, Philip?"

"Are you kidding? This is great! I mean, all this, you're sure?"

"Not all yours, you will just have to share with Kenya," she said and placed her wine glass on the windowsill and then picked up the cat walking between her ankles.

"I think I can manage. Where will you be?"

"Upstairs."

"And Oliver?"

"I don't know. Sometimes he sleeps in one of these chairs or on the couch in the first floor library."

Kenya jumped from her arms and came over to investigate me. She rubbed against my legs.

"I think you will like this room. It's warm, quiet and closest to the kitchen." She smiled and suddenly came over and gave me a hug. "I am glad you're here, Philip."

I hugged her back careful not to spill my wine down her back. She laid her head on my chest for a long moment. I closed my eyes as she seemed to melt into me there. Then, as if she suddenly remembered something she had to do, she let go, stepped back, smiled meekly up at me and left.

I took a long deep breath. It had just happened, what I had feared and hoped might.

I put my wine down on the bedside table and then lay down on the bed. Silva's presence lingered about me like a subtle perfume and opened something inside me that had been closed for a long time. I deliberately chose then to allow myself to fully remember her. The sweet smell of her hair suddenly became a doorway back to those early moments when her presence began to seep into me, and alter me it seemed, on the most basic level.

I was down in the pottery studio, in the basement of Carn Hall when the process began. It was the week before spring break. Silva was leaning over the wheel, her elegant fingers placed like tools on the clay, drawing it upwards while keeping it balanced. I could see that her many years of playing the harp had created hands well suited to her new chosen art form. She had planned to come to Westfall to play the harp in the school orchestra. She even brought her own concert size harp from England with her. I believe she had a scholarship to play for the school. And she did play and taught lessons to the younger harpists for extra money. But she had discovered in her first month at school that she loved ceramics with a passion she no longer had for the harp. It was a mistake actually. She had been forced to take ceramics due to the art history course she wanted to take being full. But it didn't take long for her to learn to throw and then after that if you ever wanted to find Silva you just went to the ceramics studio. She seemed to live there as much as Oliver lived in his closet.

I remember that day, her hair was pulled back in a pony tail and small wisps fell down about her face. There was something about her, a kind of concentration in the way she worked with the clay that I admired.

"Why must Oli always smoke? It is, if fact, against the rules, I could turn him in." I said just to make conversation.

"It keeps him awake while he paints," she said. "And you would never do such a thing Philip, you know that."

I nodded.

"And most of the smoke just goes out the window."

I nodded again.

"Looks great," I said when she was done. "I like watching you work."

"Then why don't you come visit me more often?" She said. "Not just when you get sick of Oli."

She was right. It was when Oliver was making me crazy with his enigmatic ways that I sought her out. It was because he never gave clues like Silva did, to the mystery of why they had come to America. Silva was cautious, but she would reveal some small fact if only to help me through the sometimes strange and incomprehensible ways of Oliver.

"So what shall we do about your birthday?" She asked with a flirtatious smile.

"Nothing."

"That's what I like about you Philip. You don't have many expectations."

I wasn't sure I appreciated her assessment of me, even if it rang true.

We left the ceramic studio later that night, after cleaning up, to sneak back into my dorm. I wanted to show her the latest picture Oliver had painted. When we came to my dorm I gave her ten fingers to reach up and grab the fire escape. When she pulled herself up she used my shoulders for help and for a moment her hair brushed over my face as it fell lose. It was then, with my eyes suddenly closed, that I smelled her for the first time and noticed it. She didn't know, of course, that I noticed her in this way and I didn't know what it meant for me, or how that moment would slowly grow and change how I felt about her. At the time, there was only the slightest hint of a hidden longing.

After she was up on the fire escape she waited there until I went around and checked in with my dorm parents, the Sylvesters, Joyce and Mr. Sylvester, as I called them.

"How did it go?" she said when I opened the window.

"All clear, Joyce is cool, she lets me come in late. So come on in I want you to see this painting. But be quiet. It sounds like Oli might be asleep."

She climbed in the window and we went quietly around my piles of clothes and headed for the closet door. I held her hand and it was still damp from the faucet in the ceramics studio. We came to the closet door.

"Let's see," I said. Silva nodded.

I opened the door a bit and looked into the darkness.

"Oli," Silva said gently.

Then the light went on and my eyes clamped shut. When I opened them Oliver was standing in front on us, naked, with his whole body completely covered in paint, the top half blue, the bottom half red.

"Oli," Silva said agog, "Not again!"

Oliver, in all his painted nakedness, was not exactly a nightmare, but close. I couldn't help but turn away. While I pretended not to see he explained to Silva how he had covered over an entire wall with red and blue. The latest dream was already gone. I went and found a pair of my boxers and handed them to him as I came back in the closet. Put these on, I said. He took them from me, and once he had them on he looked so absurd covered with paint that I couldn't be angry with him for covering over the painting.

Silva, on the other hand was half mad, half amused.

"Oli you shouldn't cover them up before I get to see them," She said. "And you shouldn't cover yourself in paint like that. You will poison yourself."

He made no move to apologize, and after some time of her pelting him in play with her hands and me backing away from them both, I managed to settle the mock battle by proposing I tell them a new dream.

"It will be better than the last." I promised.

"Philip is quite right, Silva," Oliver said, pushing her hands away to get at his brushes. "Let's begin again."

It was decided, and we all helped organize Oliver's paints and moved them over to the south wall, which was now dry after a couple of weeks off duty.

"Philip, what shall it be?" he asked.

I was sitting next to Silva.

"Can you paint in the dark, Oli?" Silva said.

"You know I can," he said with confidence.

"Okay then." Silva got up and flicked the lights off and then returned. She unexpectedly snuggled in next to me, and leaned her head against my shoulder. As I began my story, her hand was on my leg. Having her warmth that close, and Oliver like some animal gone mad, overwhelmed me. I got up abruptly.

"Wait," I said. "I'll be right back."

In the bathroom I threw water on my face and spent a minute looking in the mirror at my eyes. I saw the tiny yellow mountains in the blue landscape, gold pushing in towards the dark center, just like my mother's eyes. I looked at my still too pretty face. I had her smooth skin, too. It seemed I hadn't changed in years. But a part of me liked it, the youth, and wanted to stay that way forever. I was nervous and could see it in my hands. They were shaking. I suddenly remembered parts of my dream from the night before, the one I had promised them. It was filled with snow, ice, and the darkest days of winter. I had them before, these dreams, for years and I didn't like them. They made me nervous. I didn't want to talk about them at all. They were empty dreams anyway. There was nothing to paint, no colors, no horses, just a vast ominous lake covered in ice and snow where nothing lived but the howling wind.

When I went back Silva was gone. I was relieved. It gave me an excuse to get out of talking about my stupid dream.

Oliver said she had gotten herself all worried.

"About what?"

He was mixing paint at this point. "About being discovered by our dorm parents, you know."

"But, how did she leave?"

"Down the stairs, I think."

"I didn't hear her go."

Oliver ignored my question.

"Shall we begin?" He said.

He lit a small candle to see his work by. Thankfully, he still had my boxers on.

"I don't feel like it anymore. I think we should wait for Silva, maybe tomorrow night."

Oliver looked at me incredulous.

I said I was tired and that he should go on without me and paint from his own world.

"I can't Philip. I know you had a dream last night. I heard you crying in your sleep.

"That's ridiculous, I was not crying in my sleep."

"Don't act like you don't keep secrets, Philip."

"I don't. There's nothing to tell."

"Philip," he said like a parent.

"Well, okay, there are little things here and there. But why should I tell you?"

"Why else? To let go of the dead." He said pointing at my chest where the red dot from his finger still showed on my favorite shirt.

"You always avoid the dangerous stuff, Philip."

"Well, I'm sorry. I'm too tired to *share* tonight," I said.

Then I got up. But before I could leave he was in the doorway with me, half blocking me with his painted body, our faces inches apart. I could smell his breath filled with the smell of cloves that I had always loved so much.

I was unnerved, and it showed.

"Philip, I can't paint without you anymore. I need that dream."

I could hear my heart beating too fast, and I couldn't think. I slipped past him, walked into my room and over to the window.

Without turning around to look at him said, "I don't know what you're talking about."

For a long moment there was nothing, no sound from him. Then I heard him gently close the door, and for a moment I felt safe and then terribly alone.

Δ  Δ  Δ

*I am walking across the snow-covered ice. The sheriff is beside me. We are going together because I insist on going and he is my uncle Bernard's only friend. I am walking in snowshoes toward the house, following the old horse paths I know by heart, but somehow the land, the sky, the very air itself is foreign to me now. Sometimes I am completely hidden in clouds of sharp snow that rise about me and cut at my face. I find the house by way of the smoke seeping its way skyward from the chimney. There is snow surrounding the barn in wind-carved drifts, snow up beyond the first floor windows of the house, and snow bending the pine tress into perfect arcs of sadness. The horses hear me crunching the icy snow as I approach. I am a big animal walking out in a storm and it makes them nervous. They stamp and snort, but after I pass by the barn they know me by smell. Then, I stand outside the front door waiting, hoping my Uncle Bernard sees me through the kitchen window. I don't want to go into the house where my mother grew up.*

*When I open the door, he is seated in an antique chair placed in front of the wood-burning stove. He is peering over a set of old blue prints in his lap. He looks up. I don't say anything. I don't have to and can't anyway. I am frozen inside and out, forever.*

*My lips won't move. My eyes are almost closed. My uncle rises from the beautiful old chair like a giant, slowly and deliberately. Then he moves over to close the stove down tight. He takes his heavy green wool cloak down from the wall hook and walks over to me. He takes off my coat and places the cloak over my back and sits me down in his chair. The wind makes mournful sounds out of the steady river of force it sends against the house. I think that maybe she died because it is snowing. It is the snow's fault. It is the fault of the snow and the ice. It is winter's fault. This is what I try and tell him. But I cannot. I am unable to say the words, unable to speak the truth. Instead they come from somewhere else, behind me by the door, as if spoken by the wind itself. I do not hear them. I do not understand them. They are empty, meaningless words. They are a lie spoken by the howling wind.*

∆ ∆ ∆

It was my first afternoon lunch in the villa. We were all sitting around the large kitchen table next to a set of French doors, which looked out onto the vineyard. The warm stoves in the corner made the room seem close and comfortable.

The main course was bow tie pasta with artichoke hearts, peas, and trout on the side, a favorite of Carina's. Angela wasn't pleased with the trout. She seemed to think it had nothing to do with the rest of the meal. She was a demanding little woman that was clear. Her umbrella, which she brought to the table with her, looked like a giant sleeping bat, all rolled up tight waiting to unfold into the night. Angela was, indeed, an old lump of coal, all covered in layers of black embroidered cotton. She talked non-stop and seemed to be issuing forth the day's news while taking notes in a large green leather book that looked like some sort of journal or ledger. All the others asked questions except Silva who was unnaturally quiet for her.

After the news the table became a very active scene, like the dining hall at Westfall. There were several workers from the vineyard eating with us and on one level it seemed no one was really listening to anyone else, but they got the job done, the food eaten, the wine drunk. It was a real spectacle for me since they all went on in Italian and I didn't understand many words. Oliver talked to me when he spoke at all. He said it was always like this, lots of reaching for what you wanted on the table, and asking questions in the middle of a story. "That is, once Angela is done with her daily review," he said. I gathered many of them were talking about the upcoming wedding reception. I kept an eye on Silva. She listened and watched and sometimes spoke to Carina, but mostly she made herself small.

Camillo, Silva's uncle, sat leaning back in his chair with a wineglass in his hand. He looked tired and kind enough, about mid-fifties with short black hair, prominent nose and dark eyes. Oliver told me that Camillo ran the vineyard. He said that was the second largest part of Angela's operations, Silva's ceramics being the smallest, and rental properties in the village of Zagara up the hill being the largest. This estate, he said, "is about fifty acres. And Angela oversees it all with a very capable hand from what I can tell. She is quite the business woman and has been for over forty years since her husband died and she took it over."

When the conversation grew loud enough I asked Oliver quietly about Silva and her snooping for evidence of her father. As I understood it, no one knew where her father really was. But there were letters, and Silva had found them in Angela's library. Oliver said the letters were more than ten years old and all from Spain. Then Carina brought out the dessert, a carrot and walnut cake, and we had to wait until later to take up the subject. The meal ended with a white wine and then coffee, which I passed on. Instead, I retired to my room for a long nap. I didn't wake up until late and when I did the villa seemed abandoned. I found Silva and she fed me a small plate of potato gnocchi in a tomato sauce with a bit of saffron in it, to balance out the sweetness of the potatoes, she said. Then she sent me back to bed. I was still adjusting to the time change.

The next morning I awoke to beams of light tracing the white walls. I got up off the soft bed and touched my stocking feet onto the stone floor. I could feel the cold. Oliver had suggested I wear socks to sleep because if I had to exit the bed in the middle of the night I wouldn't want my bare feet touching down on the stone.

My eyes adjusted and I could make out my tidy room. Kenya was asleep on the pillow next to me. The villa was built like a fortress. I was using the deep windowsill for a shelf to put my clothes on. My journal and my pen were kept there, too.

I unhitched the window and opened it towards me, the air outside smelled good and the sunshine came through the slats of the closed storm shutters. Opening the storm shutters was trying and I had to make some heavy banging noises to accomplish it. They swung open with a thud that made me think they might not have been meant to be opened the way I did it, with force. Outside the sun was up and swaddled in a set of pale white clouds that sat up over the hill in front of me. Ten a.m. was my guess at the time, and with no rain in sight. I tried to peek out my window and over to the other windows to see if other storm shutters were open but the sill was too deep.

I could hear someone chopping wood, then a dog barked and there were some voices, distant, but talking and laughing. So as not to miss anything I got dressed. I decided not to shower because the day before, in the city, I had managed to create a water disaster area in the convent apartment when I took my first European shower. There was this old porcelain tub and a nozzle of some sort that reminded me of the spray gun located by the sink back home. There was no shower curtain. I got the water going to a warm temperature while I stood on the cold tile floor. It was a bathroom with a chill too severe for a naked body. I stepped into the tub carefully because it looked slick. I stood there naked for a while with the nozzle spraying down at my feet. I didn't understand how to use it. Apparently, one is supposed to sit and spray not stand. But it seemed ridiculous at the time, sit and spray.

"No curtain," I thought. "How odd."

Then I noticed that the entire bathroom was white ceramic tile, walls and all, and I figured everyone stood up to spray and just let the water fly since it wouldn't harm anything.

I was wrong, of course.

The water started flowing out from the under the door and by that time I heard Silva calling to Oliver. I wasn't looking anymore. It was too late.

"Oliver! God! Come help Philip with the shower. We are having a flood!"

So Oliver walked right in. He didn't ask. Sometimes, back in school, I would forget he was in the closet and he would inevitably walk out as I was either putting on or taking off my clothes. He would talk to me like that, me leaning over with boxers at my knees, or some other equally embarrassing pose. Later, after I got used to it, I would keep dressing in front of him since he didn't seem to care one way or the other.

"What are you trying to do to us, Philip?"

At that point my hair was a tower of foam and I had already managed to drop the spray nozzle into the tub which, when I felt it drop from my hand nearly made me slip on my own suds as I tried to keep my toes safe. I figured once it was down there that the sprayer was doing fine on its own since it was in the tub. But the sprayers of the world have more power when they are down at the level where they are supposed to be used. The spray was arching up like a fountain and landing on the tile floor, soft as spring rain. It might have sounded nice if I could have heard it but my ears were filled with soap bubbles.

"Sit! You need to sit when you bathe," Oliver yelled.

I was not amused. Then I heard Silva's laugh coming from behind him. It wasn't standing there naked that bothered me so much--I was used to it with Oliver around--but being blinded, mostly deaf, and scared I would slip on the porcelain, and knowing Silva was looking me over, was too much.

"Thank you, both. Now, could you lend a hand, then perhaps vacate," I said.

There were hands and lots of directions and I was helped down. I felt water being sprayed on my head, hands washing out the soap in my hair. The sprayer was hitting me with warmth and making strange squeaking noises that came up through the pipes. I couldn't talk because of the water and soap going down my face.

After a moment Silva said, "Okay, you're safe, open your eyes."

Oliver had thrown some towels on the floor and was swishing them around in wide arcs with his foot and holding onto the door with one hand so he wouldn't fall. Silva was squatting next to the tub with the sprayer in her hand and smiling salaciously at me. I washed my hands, rubbed my eyes while turning red at the neck.

"I will take baths from now on and use the sprayer thing only as an accessory," I said.

She nodded her approval and then placed her hand on my cheek like I was a little boy, which is exactly how I felt.

Instead of another attempt at a shower I just washed my face and headed outside to find the others. I went to the kitchen first. Breakfast food was scarce it seemed. I scrounged up the left over bread and cheese--but I found nothing of true morning sustenance. I was not pleased with the prospect of going without an American breakfast of eggs, bacon, etc. Breakfast is my only true culinary requirement. I searched for the refrigerator and couldn't find it, figured on it being in another room and still couldn't find it.

I finally tried melting cheese on some bread in the brick oven. The coals were low but a little limpness passed into the cheese and I managed to get down two slices before Angela walked in silently behind me while my mouth was full and suddenly felt it necessary to yell out "Philip!" I turned around quickly as you can imagine, petrified that I had broken some sort of Italian food taboo. I looked at the old matriarch with my eyebrows held high and a guilty smile over my bulging mouth.

"This house is no good for you," she said wagging her finger back and forth at me. "This house, very bad…for you," she said pointing precisely at the red dot on my shirt, the very same one that Oliver had created that first day in the closet and which I had donned in honor of my return to my old best friends.

Her eyes were giving off that vague beam of light consisting of a motherly disapproval and yet some sort of concern as well. She just waited there, hand on umbrella. Then she smiled a big fully toothed smile. So I nodded and smiled back until she chuckled, shrugged her shoulders and then made her way out of the kitchen back to whatever realm she regularly inhabited. She seemed like a caricature of a witch except for all those gleaming white false teeth she had. I liked her little shrug, like we had just shared some private joke.

After Angela's departure I washed the bread down with water and then I looked out the sink window and saw a massive patio that was half the size of a tennis court. Silva, Camillo, and Carina were having some sort of breakfast at a white iron wrought table by the far edge of the patio that looked out over the valley below. Oliver was nowhere to be seen. There was coffee on the table out there. I could almost smell it. A cat was wandering around the patio and another sat sunning itself on the wooden railing that defined the edge of the patio and the drop-off beyond. I went out and they all welcomed me. I enjoyed a light breakfast of zucchini fritters with lemon, which Silva said Carina made just for my American needs. I felt embarrassed that I had assumed she wouldn't know how to take care of me and ate the fritters with so much gusto she offered to make another round. I declined but said they were fantastic like Oliver like to say about Carina's cooking.

Then Silva suggested she give me the full tour of the Villa and the estate. I agreed. We started out in the kitchen. She showed me the door beyond which a refrigerator stood, for which I was thankful. It was a massive restaurant walk-in with two sides, one freezer and one refrigerator. There was everything from chocolate to scallops. If something was needed it would be there, stocked and well organized by Carina.

"Carina is a zealot for preparation," Silva said. We were looking and poking about in the fridge for a small dessert item for the road. "Her catering is the best, she is quite famous in the city. She has people coming up here for weekends all through the spring, summer and early fall, unless it rains so much like this year."

"Does she have any children?" I asked and closed the heavy metal door with a snap.

"They're in Bologna, at the university. They come back here most weekends, sometimes to help with the work, but mostly to pick up the food she has made for them. La Mama provides for her boys" Silva said smiling.

"I see. And you?" I asked as we made our way down a hall to the great room.

"What about me?"

"You and Carina?"

"I help her sometimes and in exchange she is making me into a good Italian cook. And I like to do it. She...well...I think she understands me better than the rest, and she doesn't have any daughters."

"She seems to like you."

Silva turned and smiled at me.

We kept walking down the corridor until she stopped and said into the air in front of us. "I don't ever want to become like Angela."

I can't say I understood exactly what that meant, but I put my hand briefly on her back in support.

Then she took me through all of the first floor rooms in the villa. The ground floor had two complete apartments, one for Carina whose husband had died years ago and one for Camillo who never married. There were three guest rooms including mine that once were used by Carina's children, a sewing room, library, the kitchen-dining room, the great hall, and the burnt room which once was used for wood storage until a few years ago when it had had been lost in blaze of unknown origin. It was still all black from the smoke.

We never explored the top floor of the house.

"Those are Angela's rooms, and my room," she said, "and please Philip, don't go searching for things up there. Angela gets very upset if people go poking around."

"You should know."

"I only warn you because I know how you love to explore, and around here it costs more than it did in Westfall when you get caught."

"But I never got caught."

"True, but you didn't have a witch in the dorm with you."

"And what about yourself?"

"So, Oliver told you about how I *discovered* the letters."

I nodded.

"Well, I suspected they all knew more than they were telling me, and so I just looked. I had a legitimate reason to search her office and was proved right," she said firmly.

I didn't like disagreeing with her when she used that tone of voice so I nodded again.

We took a brisk walk through the wine cellar where Camillo often worked. Its vast network of rooms held barrel after barrel of wine and a few large tanks where the fermenting took place. We walked by them and down a long sloping cave-like tunnel. She said we were under the patio, going through the hill itself. It felt very medieval. When we arrived at our destination it was Silva's studio. Light came in through a set of grated arches. It was a basement with long tables and new shelves with a few exits into passages that led down somewhere deeper.

"Quite a place, Silva."

"Sure, but it's cold as hell down here and damp, and I don't really have everything I need. Some of the stuff is old and doesn't work. She looked around and didn't seem content with the studio, not like she had been in Westfall. We walked outdoors into the gardens to where an old dilapidated wood-fired kiln was sitting. Silva had been trying to rebuild it until recently.

"Where are you firing then?"

"In a small electric upstairs. I was rebuilding this." She pointed to the large six-chambered kiln to the left, which flowed down the hill like an undulating worm.

"The problem here is that wood is too expensive and to get a gas hook up will be too expensive, too. But if I stay, finish at the university, and commit to being here, then Angela says she will put a gas kiln in. But I don't know. I just..." She shook her head.

"It sounds like she's trying to help."

"Yes, but it's always the people who help that seem to hold me back, in my best interest, of course. They tell me to leave my father alone. They make it sound like it should be easy. She's just like my mother always telling me to stop living in a fantasy world."

I was silent as we walked down a stone path through some waterlogged gardens to a lookout spot.

"So, what do you really know about your father?"

"Camillo told me some things. But I don't believe them. I think they are just trying to make him out to be a monster so I will give up on him like they all have."

"You don't know much then?"

"No, just that after he took me to Africa he went to Northern Spain and never came back. I guess they don't like him because he ditched on his family responsibilities. He was the eldest son and was supposed to stay here and run the vineyard for the family. Camillo is actually a doctor but gave up his seven year old practice in the city to run the place for Angela when my father left. I don't blame Camillo for being angry. He still has an office and does medicine in the village for free, but that's it. It's Angela I blame. I suspect she drove my father away somehow after my parents divorce. She doesn't really ever let up on her control of this place or anyone living here. She owns it all so she has the final say on everything. It's tiring sometimes."

"I can imagine," I said. "And she's a witch as well right," I said trying to lighten things up.

Silva laughed, "Yes, she has a sort of gift for predictions."

We stood looking out over the gardens as they flowed down the hillside and eventually into a grove of olive trees. It was a beautiful view. I remembered then how Oliver had once told me the story of Silva's father. He had essentially stolen Silva away after the divorce and taken her to Africa: Egypt actually. Silva had believed it was going to be a vacation, but Oliver told me it was more like a kidnapping. Her father hadn't told anyone he was going. He had lost custody of her and this was his answer. The police and her mother finally caught up with him and took her away.

"Philip, has Oliver spoken to you yet?" Silva said suddenly.

"About what?"

She didn't answer.

"What is it?"

"It's nothing really. He just has something he wants to say to you, and he made me swear not to tell you first."

"Really? What is it?"

"I can't tell you, Philip, really. I promised him, " she said smiling.

"What's the big deal?"

"He just thinks you'll be sensitive on the issue. I told him you would be fine, but he still thinks back to Westfall, you know, how things ended."

"Yes, well. That was then."

"That's what I told him," she said turning to agree with me.

"Come on, let's walk," she said taking my hand for a moment to get me to follow her.

We moved along an old path across the shoulder of the hill. When we rounded a brick shed we came upon a steep drop that looked over a sloping field. She pointed out the new games area for the summer guests, a horse shoe court, baci court, and a court for some game I had never seen before. There was a small pool, above ground. I was surprised to find that it contained fish. Trout, she said. I was allowed to fish for lunch if I wanted, she said, but it didn't excite me, fishing for trout that don't have much of a choice but to be caught. We left behind the trout and made our way up a tiny path behind the villa towards the village of Zagara. The walk wasn't easy so I went slow so as not to exhaust myself for whatever we might climb next. I noticed Silva's legs, not for the first time. She was wearing skin-tight black stretch pants that clung to her curves. She looked strong.

We didn't talk all the way up, mostly because she out-paced me in a matter of minutes. I began to wonder about what she had said earlier. I wasn't so sure I even wanted to know what Oliver had to say to me. At least not before I had told him a few things myself. I couldn't have him beating me to a confession. There were things from the past we needed to discuss. Telling him the truth was one of the real reasons I had come to Italy. At least that was what I told myself.

We stopped a short distance from the small walled medieval village of Zagara that perched on top the hill like a crown. She showed me a secluded bench beneath a tree and we sat down there not far from the village wall. Silva said this was a place lovers had been meeting for three centuries. At least that was the legend in the town. And she said the small hidden path we had taken to get up to the village had been used in World War II by the resistance. Some villagers, she said, knew how to travel south to Florence all through the hills without being seen. I was glad to hear it, but not interested in learning their secrets just yet.

"It would take us a few days I think," she said looking serious about the trip.

I looked back down the path. "Maybe we could do the trip on horses." I suggested.

Suddenly she sat up straight. She seemed thrilled about the idea of getting away, of escape. Then she spilled out a whole series of details about how we could manage the journey. I contributed here and there and we talked and planned for about ten minutes. Then she looked out over the trail and I saw there was something alive and true flashing in her eyes. It was something I loved about her, the light in her eyes. It reminded me of the first time I had seen it. We were back in school and I had been looking for her all day. I found her in the middle of the soccer field at dusk. Fireflies were rising up out of the grass and moving through the air like illuminated flakes of snow. She was circling and spinning around with them, dancing in the way one can when only the invisible world is watching. I had been teaching her to dance the waltz in the few weeks after Oliver's accident and here she was practicing it by herself, her arms out, waiting for her partner.

I walked up through fireflies and when she saw me she danced and twirled over in my direction. Her hair was flying about her in wispy tails, her jeans covered in clay, and her Westfall sweatshirt was dashed with glazes where she had wiped her hands. She was just about as beautiful a thing as I had ever seen.

I stood in position with my arms out. She spun herself into place and after a moment's pause in which the sweet smell of her hair floated over me, we began.

We were dancing well without trying, but every now and then we lost the balance when she tried to break into my lead and take over. It was the biggest hurdle for her in dancing, letting me lead. It was in her character to be in control. It was part of what I liked about her. But I couldn't teach her if she wouldn't let me, and bit by bit she had let go over the last few lessons. But she still sometimes reverted, as if there were a muscle for dominance in her personality that would relax for a moment and then suddenly jerk into gear again and throw us out of balance. We would have to stop and begin again, she apologizing and embarrassed.

I remember I said that it was not a problem, that it takes time to learn the art of surrender. "You can't try and surrender, it has to happen before you know it," I said.

It was something my mother had said to me over and over when she taught me to dance.

Suddenly as if my words were magic, we were gliding through mist and tiny floating lights, like two breezes talking together. We looked in each other's eyes and smiled, amazed at ourselves and the calm intensity that was with us. Perfect balance and perfect timing are rare at any moment in life, but having it with another person, even for a moment, well, I think it is almost the most beautiful thing that can happen between two people.

We sat on the lover's bench for some time and talked in greater depth about our plans to ride horses to Florence. It was a trip I knew we would never take but which as we dreamed it up together, transported us to a world where everything danced with perfect balance and perfect timing. We talked like this until our vision for the trip was distilled, and we both were sweetly convinced we would indeed make that journey together, someday, soon. A gentle satisfaction settled over us both. One that lingered with us through the silence that followed our shared dream.

Then, after a while, we talked about other things. We talked about Westfall and what had happened to each of us since then. I told her a little about my friends Jake, Claudia and Andre from back at Boston College. She talked about how much she had missed Oliver while he traveled around the world for three years on his own. How she wished she could have been with him herself. Then, somehow we ended up speaking about how she and Oliver had come to be together and that fateful trip to Africa she took with her father. Things we had never really spoken of before in any depth.

"I was only seven," she said. " And when they brought me home it was already over, their marriage. Can you believe it? I thought we were just on vacation, like he said, and that my mother was going to meet us there, in Africa."

"It wasn't how I had imagined it would be. My parents had been talking about Africa for years and all my toys were African animals. I thought the place was one big zoo. But it was nothing but people when we got there, people always rushing us here and there and us acting like we were running from something. It was fun at first, you know, a game. My father was always telling me we were going to see the animals, soon, very soon. But I never did get to see them."

She couldn't remember much more except that when the police arrived, her father simply vanished. He left her sitting at a cafe table when he saw the police car roll in with her mother in it.

"He said he would come back for me. Then he ran across the plaza and around the corner of a building. And that, him running away, I will never forget," she said.

She never saw him again after that.

I looked over at Silva and could see in her eyes that she was resisting letting it go. I had never seen her cry and it seemed she never wanted me to because she held it back like she did so many things.

"What about Oliver?" I said changing the subject for her.

"Oh, he wasn't there yet," she said getting herself back together.

"The only good thing about any of it was Oliver. You see, Oli, myself, my mother, and my new ugly middle-class stepfather Sol were suddenly all living in this huge old house together in London. I never went back home to Italy after they found me and my mother never spoke about my father, or Italy, none of it. Like it was all some dream. I suppose it took weeks for it all to transpire but I can't remember the transition. It seemed like the world simply vanished and began again somewhere else, and I was the only one who remembered any of it. That's when I started to get ill. I couldn't hold down any food. At meals Sol would give me this disgusted look and swear when it happened—my mother would get mad at me too. They took me to see doctors. She said I was becoming an embarrassment, puking all over like that. Once I even did it on the Persian carpet. She never forgave me for that, she said I did it on purpose. Who knows maybe I did. But I was in a strange house, surrounded by strange people and food. They deserved it. It wasn't my fault. But I wouldn't have known that it if it weren't for Oliver. He just sat across from me at the table watching it all with this pathetic look on his face. Then later, at night, he'd sneak toast up to the loft for me to eat real slowly so as not to make a mess all over the bed. Oliver was the only reason I survived at all."

"You were lucky you had someone," I said.

She looked out over the valley and the trail again. "Yes, I was," she said slowly, as if wondering where Oliver was at that very moment.

"We should get going," she said suddenly.

On the way back to the villa we didn't talk much. I thought about the losses we both carried inside us and how we quite honestly didn't know what to do with them, or how to make them stop happening to us over and over in some subdued fashion. I thought also about some of the last days we had spent together back at school. These were the times we had been avoiding talking about, when events had seemingly taken on a life of their own, and all any of us could do was play out our parts and be bitten once again by the same old loss.

Δ   Δ   Δ

After Oliver was finally let out of the Westfall infirmary I began thinking up a plan to keep them both with me for the summer. Oliver and Silva, I had to keep them with me. They were my best friends and the only true friends I had ever really had as far as I was concerned. Despite what I had been telling myself for the three years before they arrived, being alone with one's books and studies was not all it was cracked up to be.

Since Oliver had been back in the dorm room with me, I had refrained from working on any new dream-paintings with him, as I had promised Silva. She was nervous about him overworking himself. She said he was still not right, and maybe never would be. His skin looked more sallow than normal and he had lost weight.

Oliver had tried to get me to start, but I had a good reason to hold him off. By then I was unknowingly in love with Silva and would have done anything she asked. I am sure she knew this long before I did. So I just made excuses to Oliver and myself that I was too busy studying for my exams to dream or paint. So he went on painting without me, and I conveniently forgot to tell Silva he was working on his own in the closet.

I had been mulling my plan over in my head to give it shape and possibility. I was imagining the relief filled summer days I would have with Oliver and Silva up on the horse farm with me. The three of us would be there together, making dream-pictures. I sat by Silva at lunch one day a few weeks before graduation and promised her she would get to Italy some day if I had anything to do with it.

She turned and smiled at me sweetly.

"Thank you Philip," she said.

"So why don't you stay with me this summer, the both of you. You can save some money and work with me on the horse farm. That way you won't have to go back to England."

She waited a moment. "That's sweet of you Philip. I will talk to Oliver about it," she said sort of stiffly. It was unlike her to use her stuffy English upbringing on me like that. Something was bothering her but I was too afraid to ask what.

May fifth, graduation day Oliver appeared on the stage in the same baggy white linen clothes he had arrived in. He wore a painted leather patch of blue and red designs over his glass eye. Silva had wanted him to be at graduation desperately. Oliver had resisted. He meant to graduate in silence and anonymity if possible. "I do not like public rituals," he said.

But Silva insisted despite his condition. I tried not to get involved in the argument much because I knew I couldn't think clearly about what was best for him.

"Oli, you must be recognized for your talent. You, Philip, of all people should understand that." She had turned on me because she sensed my silence meant that I was for Oliver not receiving his diploma in public. I nodded my assent to Silva, then said, "Oliver, you really should."

In the end, Silva won, and Oliver was the star of the day. He achieved standing applause and Silva was right, it was important he went, for she had known he was going to receive a full scholarship to go to art school at Cooper Union in New York City the next fall. Some of the Westfall Academy Alumni had arranged it without Oliver even knowing. In addition, the Association would pay for his living expenses. I remember him looking extremely uncomfortable up on the stage despite his sudden success and elegant linen clothes, which Silva had neatly pressed for the occasion. It was clear he didn't like the attention. He said only one word, "Thanks," and then vanished from view as soon as he could get off the stage.

Our time at Westfall came to an end with this small but important victory for Silva and Oliver. I felt reassured that Oliver would be going to school in New York. I offered to them again my plan for their summer. Silva still hadn't given me a straight answer. She had been avoiding it for weeks, ever since I mentioned it to her. But I was sure she would come around. She said again that she would have to speak to Oliver because he was still unsure. I hadn't spoken to Oliver about it myself. I wanted to let her handle it her own way. She was extremely protective of him after he had the eye removed. Plus, I had the feeling that Oliver didn't want to think about the future too much. But it made me anxious, them not telling me what their plans were. I had seen he and Silva talking once while they were walking down to the river, and I assumed they were discussing my offer. I would be patient, I thought. After the graduation party at my house, they naturally would just stay on. It was the obvious choice. Where else would they go.

Δ Δ Δ

The next morning Silva said over breakfast on the vast patio.

"I'm shopping for the wedding reception today," do you want to go along."

I said I wanted to stay at the villa, that I had some writing I needed to do. She smiled and reached up to place her hand on my cheek like she had done after my shower disaster back at the convent.

"Are you having fun Philip?" She said as she held her hand there gently.

"Yes, don't worry about me. I just need a little private time today."

"Okay," she said, then kissed me on both cheeks and left.
Actually I wanted to talk with Oliver alone. I did have some writing in my journal to do as well, but I didn't do any of it. I went back to my room and instead of writing I took the shark's tooth Oliver had given me out of my bag and I held it up to the light. I turned it around and then lay it on the bedside table. Then I picked up an Italian fashion magazine. I pieced together a very few things from the Latin I had studied. Mostly I looked at the pictures of the beautiful people. Then I fell asleep on the bed for a while and dreamed about the horse riding trip Silva and I had imagined we would take to Florence. In it we were lovers. Not because we actually had sex in the dream. I could tell just by the way she looked at me as we rode along the secret trails that lead south.

When I woke up I went to the kitchen where there was a mid morning snack of lemon scones. I suddenly realized I was eating much more than was normal for me. But I couldn't help myself. I was nervous. I had an uneasy feeling inside me that there wouldn't be enough at the main meals, which was never the case. Maybe it was Silva, and the dream and such. All I knew is that whenever possible I availed myself of Carina's generosity. Oliver on the other hand, when he showed up in the kitchen soon after me, didn't seem interested in food much. He said hello and then went into the great hall and stoked up the fire. I followed him in and we sat at one end of the huge oak banquet table and played a game of chess.

Oliver sketched while we played. Whenever I was busy deciding my next move he took up his book and let his hand flow over the page. He was drawing the game. Our first game ended in a stalemate. Then Oliver disappeared upstairs for a moment while I set up the pieces for another game. The chessboard was a fine marble one with a crack running through it which had somehow been glued back together. I wondered what the story behind it was, what had run amuck in order to break a marble board.

Oliver came back with a bottle of dark rum.

"Drinks?"

It was early yet but I was game.

"Sure," I said.

He went into the kitchen to fetch something to go with the rum. I heard glasses clink. I went outside for a few logs while he made our drinks. They didn't have the easy burning split wood like I was used to in the States. They used whatever they could get their hands on. Fallen branches, stumps, or anything left over after a storm. It all made for awkward carrying.

In the carriage house I unexpectedly saw Angela. She was settling Husband into his stall after his morning walk. I sneaked past and into the wood shed. I didn't feel like meeting her alone again. Words floated over through some hidden hole in the wall. Italian muttering I couldn't even guess at.

I was holding a large stump in my arms at the moment I heard her call what sounded like my name. I froze. Her high voice gave a charge to the air. I walked, stump in arms, out my door and in the other hoping she would see I was busy and leave me alone.

She wasn't there.

I looked in the stall. Husband looked back at me. His eyes were pink and blind as a newborn puppy.

"You see anyone, Husband?" I asked.

Nothing, absolutely no recognition of my presence, even when I stuck my face up close to his nose. But he knew I was there. I could tell by his attitude.

"Loyal to the end, eh, Husband?"

I waited another minute while the stump grew heavy in my arms. I looked about a bit. Nothing. No way out the back of the stables. I checked. This crone of a woman was perplexing to me. She was aloof, always somewhat edgy, and yet there was an unspoken recognition that she was the supreme power behind this place. The entire villa exuded and perfectly matched the small crumpled matriarch's odd presence. I could ignore it most of the time, but every now and then, when I was alone in a hallway or room, I felt that presence, as if she were watching me, or waiting for something to happen to me. I wrote it off to that moment in the kitchen the day before when we had shared that little surprise and odd but kind laughter. I was being paranoid. Maybe it was just the age of the entire place; too many ghosts floating about.

I walked through the door, turned right, and headed back into the main hall. Oliver had already made his first move, and two glasses of what looked like rum and coke were set up. I put the stump down carefully. It thumped lightly on the floor and then rolled into the fire a bit. I stood up and stretched my back.

"Did you see Angela come in?" I asked.

"No."

"I thought I heard her call my name."

"Did you answer her?"

"No, it sort of unnerves me just seeing her around let alone talking with her."

Oliver came over to help me roll the stump into place.

"Why? She's harmless enough."

"Well, she made a sort of prophecy the other morning that this house was no good for me."

Oliver raised his eyebrows at me.

"Here, let's roll this wood in and get it going," he said, leaning over to get a hand on it.

There we were, shoulder to shoulder. We got the wood situated back in the enormous fire place.

Oliver looked at me with his one eye.

"You know Philip, Angela made a similar statement to me about Silva before she started snooping around in the office upstairs. She told me to watch Silva, that she was likely to soon get herself in trouble. I couldn't get much more out of her. Her English is really limited, but when I talked with Carina about it she said Angela was usually right about such things. "

"Really?"

"Sure, she knew Silva and I were coming over from the States before Silva even called her. Carina proved it, she showed me that day journal in which Angela writes down everything about the villa and the business, including little notes about her predictions. I saw it right there in black a white, *lost grand child coming soon.* It was in Italian of course, but then turn the page and four days later, there it is, a note that Silva had called from America to arrange a visit. She knew we were coming before we even did. They all did in fact. That's why she does all that writing in front of everyone at lunch. So she doesn't have everyone doubting her intuition at every seemingly odd decision or pronouncement she makes."

"That's crazy."

"Maybe, but it's effective. She has been running this place and pretty much the village as well ever since her husband died and no one else wants the job. She's too successful."

Oliver stood up and walked back to the chess board.

"You're probably in there too," he said.

"Really?"

"I would guess."

"Where is it."

"In the off limits office upstairs so don't even think about it. Carina can get it for you if you really want."

"No, that's okay. I don't want to know. But what do you think it's about, her warning."

"I don't know, anything could happen Philip. Now make your move."

I looked at the chess board and made a move quickly.

"Silva said you had something you needed to tell me?" I said as he made his next move.

"Really." He said looking surprised.

"Yes."

"Well, nothing but that I would like to sketch and do a portraits of you."

"That's it."

"Yeah."

"She made it seem more...important."

"Maybe there's your trouble Philip. Silva always has a hidden agenda of some sort."

"Maybe."

"So will you come and sit for me soon?" He asked.

"Well...I'm not sure I want to be drawn and covered up just yet."

"It's okay, Philip. I understand. You're just not ready yet. It can be an awkward process. Just let me know."

It was a perfect excuse he gave me.

"You don't mind if I start with Silva then, before you?" he said.

"No, sure, go ahead," I said.

"Excellent, I didn't want you to be angry with me for starting with her."

He smiled and took the time to lift his eye patch and rub his crippled eyelid over his glass eye. I felt my shoulders relax. "Sometime, we should start another dream-painting, Philip. What do you say?"

"Yes, we should, that would be good."

"You know we never did finish the one we began back in Westfall before my eye accident."

"What was it we were doing then? I can't remember."

"Think about it," and he looked at the chessboard and my last move.

"Nothing?" He asked?

I couldn't summon it forth. I had instead another image, something I thought we had finished before the accident. "I just see a horse scene, the one...."

"Yes, I remember that one. I used some of those images in another work which sold in London last year."

"Really?"

"Absolutely, I told you it would all come back and be better. Your influence is scattered all through my work Philip, an image here and there. Many of the paintings are partially from your dreams and they are as vivid and detailed as when you told them to me."

"Are they all covered over, too?"

"No, I really only do that with the portraits. I am after the soul and truth of people and so cover the form in order to find it after I have them sketched."

"Your work is selling in London too?"

"Yes, and London and Milan is enough for now."

Then Oliver suddenly looked concerned.

"What's wrong Oli?"

"Nothing really, I just feel tired. I guess the rum is getting to me. I am going to take a nap. Let me know when you are ready for a portrait Phillip, we only have a few days left with you here, okay?

"Okay," I said. "What about our match here."

"I concede this one," he said.

"You sure?"

He nodded. "We'll play again later."

Then he left for the upper bedrooms and I went off through the side door that led to my room. I was half-worried and half-pleased when I lay down on the bed. I had avoided the portrait which unnerved me as much as Angela's little prophecy. Oliver had some deeper reason for wanting to paint me that I had not gathered yet. But whatever it was my gut didn't like it. Oliver didn't look well for one thing. He seemed lethargic and lazy, something I had never before seen in him, and the special grace and ease within which he had moved through the world seemed diminished. Something was bothering him beyond being tired and beyond whatever Silva's intentions might be for him or myself. I knew Silva wanted something from me and him but I was unsure what. That was not unexpected. I would just have to let her get to it on her own. I had my own agenda after all.

I might have fallen asleep blissfully then, but a silence filled the villa. I felt I was the only person there, maybe the only person for miles around. So instead of sleep I fell into memories of the summers I spent in Vermont working on my uncles' heavy horse farm. Perhaps it was hearing about how my dreams were strewn about and woven into Oliver's work that got me remembering. I had never understood how much I had become a part of Oliver or his work.

I remembered there was a stretch of three summers where it seems like all I did was play chess with my mother. When times were sluggish and the August humidity was wilting the very air we breathed, out came chess board. She would let me win sometimes, even though she was a virtual chess master compared to me.

I remembered then what the dream Oliver and I had never finished painting was all about. We had decided to do it, the two of us, to paint the chess pieces and the ballroom dancing that were my mother's magic and had been appearing in my dreams during the weeks before he lost his eye. Oliver, in a sense, had been waking up my memories, one by one, in those last few days before he was hurt, of the life I had had with my mother before she died. Then, after the accident, it all stopped, the dreams about my mother, and the paintings on the closet walls, all of it. It felt as if everything had just suddenly frozen up because of the accident and that we had left something important unfinished.

Δ  Δ  Δ

It was just a half hour after the Westfall graduation. Oliver had vanished and Silva said she was heading down to the studio to pick up some of her last pieces. I decided to ask her again about staying on for the summer with me up in Vermont and saving some money.  She didn't even wait for me to ask. She said she and Oli were going to Italy. That she had sold her concert harp to the school to raise the money. In one gesture, she had done away with everything I cared about. Her harp was worth more than enough to pay for the trip she said, and then some.

"It had to be done, Philip. I had to make a choice between ceramics and the harp. I brought the harp with me intending to become a professional but ceramics has become my true love. Plus, I want to go to Italy to look for my real father more than I want to give harp lessons."

She said thank you, too, for the offer to stay the summer with me. She and Oliver would take me up on it some other time. She had worked it all out. She had had to make choice and her trip to Italy was more important. I was calm and pretended to be okay with it. I said I understood. But I didn't, or didn't want to. But I hid it well, my disappointment, which I was especially good at doing, so much so that people thought I was unattached or untouched by such things. But this was a lie. I made for the exit as quick as possible to avoid revealing the truth.

I walked home quickly, by myself. When I came out of the woods and up to my back porch I saw him there, Oliver, in one of our white Aderondack chairs. I sat in the other one next to him in silence for a while, preparing for my last best hope at keeping him here and returning us to what we had before the accident.

I looked around at the oaks, hemlocks, and maples in the yard. They had turned leafy, and I had been too busy worrying about Oliver and Silva, and choosing between the colleges I wanted to attend to notice. It would be Boston College for me. I was satisfied with that part of my life. I had decided I wanted a bigger school I could easily lose myself in. Silva's departure was just days away, she had told me. But I was not convinced yet that Oliver would abandon me and follow her on the quest.

Oliver and I decided to go down along the river to collect twigs for kindling in the woods that separated my house from the school's land. The graduation party was to be that night and we needed wood.

The celebration had been easy to plan. Silva had a lot of friends. "Invite the whole school," was what my father had said.

"Put them all in the back yard, make a fire in the pit. Do whatever you like."

It had been too many years since the house had been full of life. Oliver and I were talking together about whom we might have missed with the invitations when I interrupted him.

"So, you're going to Italy?" I said.

"I don't think so. We don't have the money." He was busying himself down by the ground, picking up a branch while his one good eye was turned away from me so I was unsure if he was serious or not. I wondered if he could not know about the recent turn in their economic situation.

"What about your parents?"

"They want us to fly back to London and then go to University there."

"What about New York, for you."

"They don't know about the scholarship yet. I haven't called them."

"But they will be okay with that since it costs them nothing. But they will refuse to help Silva go to Italy. I don't know what she's going to do."

"So you didn't know that Silva sold her harp?"

"What?"

"I just assumed you knew."

Oliver looked stunned. "No!" He said, looking amazed. "I assumed we were staying with you, like you said. I've just been putting off telling my parents."

"You didn't know?"

"No."

"How can she do that? With the harp?" I asked. "Is it hers?"

"It was a gift to her from her grandmother, Angela in Italy. She can do whatever she wants with it, but, she didn't tell me yet. Maybe she just heard from the school that they would buy it in the same way I got my scholarship. Its an excellent instrument. I'm not surprised they bought it."

Oliver was missing my intention.

I turned and stood opposite of him and made him look at me. "Well then, you come with me to the island. I mean...you could paint. There are lots of things we could do. My uncle will pay us. You can save money for next year. I think it could work."

"Philip," he said slowly.

"What?"

He didn't go on but just looked at me and smiled.

I knew what it meant. It made me feel silly for showing how much I wanted him to stay. I started searching for more twigs. He followed and in a few minutes we had enough wood gathered to take back to the small stone ringed earth pit in the center of the back yard.

"I'm going to be rebuilding the barn this year with my Uncle," I said seriously as we walked along. We dumped our twigs into the fire pit.

"We could use your help."

"I think that's enough," he said.

"I'm sorry."

"No, I mean wood. It's enough wood. Don't you think?"

The pile was big enough.

"Sure," I said let's go back.

When we got back to the grassy yard we stood there for an awkward minute at the edge. It was in good shape, the yard. My father had risen early and mowed the entire back lawn, waking everyone up in the neighborhood with the noise. A breeze came in carrying the smell of cut grass. It wrestled lightly with Oliver's short ragged hair. He looked over at me. I looked at him. It wasn't something I did very much, looking right at him, in his real eye. I could look at his patch easily enough. I did it often. He had a dozen of them by then, all with elaborate and beautiful designs painted on them. His patches were his first real attempt to work after the infirmary and I had encouraged him by buying numerous varieties for him to choose from. Some of them he had even painted false eyes onto, large colorful Italian eyes, and sleepy looking Asian eyes. He experimented until he had a whole set of possibilities to choose from on any given day.

"It's just that I feel responsible, Oli," I said.

"I don't want to hear any of that nonsense about your code of responsibility, Philip."

I let a long stretch pass. "Yes, I suppose..." I said.

"Now, if I came. Could I paint, for sure?"

He let the question sit there in the air before us. I let it sit there, too. The sunlight was draped along the moving surface of the river, and birds sailed their pale shadows across from bank to bank in perfect arcs.

"You could."

He touched me then, on the shoulder, and I think for the first time ever it did not make my insides tremble.

"And Silva?" I asked.

"I'll talk with her. Maybe we can work something out. Maybe we can have it all Philip, you and Vermont as well as Italy."

"Could that work?"

"It might," he said. Then, after a pause where he seemed to ponder some hidden complications I was unaware of, he said, "I'm going for the lighter fluid."

I remained standing there for a moment in silence with the wood in my arms. In the distance I heard him groping around the tool shed for liquid flammables. The river before me was flowing high and for a long moment I felt like things would go my way.

Then I heard him in the shed again and I wondered what was taking him so long. I should have known. It was dark in there and he had lost depth perception with the accident. He was probably bumping into things all over. I lay down the wood and went to help him.

Δ  Δ  Δ

That afternoon it was raining, but I decided to take a walk anyway after rummaging through my suitcase for the umbrella I had brought with me. I headed out the cobblestone drive that ended at the thin paved road. Right across from the drive was a small chapel that the wedding would take place in. I took a left and wandered down the road. I had reviewed much of those last days with Oliver and Silva and still, all these years later I was unsure of what went wrong, of why Silva felt she had to leave me. I was sure I was missing some part of a larger puzzle. Finding out what it could have been, was part of the reason I had come to Italy. If I had done something to cause me to lose the only true friends I ever had I wanted to know what it was, even three years later.

I was standing by a stream that was overflowing and rushing across the street when Camillo drove up the hill toward me. He stopped the car and I got in. He was on his way up to Zagara for some things so I rode along with him and we talked a bit. I don't remember how but we ended up talking about Silva, her father and mother, and the entire debacle of their marriage, but we did. Camillo's English wasn't perfect, but it was sufficient for the task.

"I thought Angela should have told her right away, the truth," he said, "that he is in Spain, and alive."

I opened the window because he was smoking and my lungs already felt thick from all the rain and walking.

"Then she will find him someday," I said.

"I know where," he said and looked ahead leaning over the wheel looking for the road. Camillo said he had spoken with an old medical school friend recently who traveled the world helping the poor and who said he had seen Silva's father in Barcelona just a few months ago working in a hospital.

"Why haven't you told her?"

"It is a delicate thing. Her father, he stayed away for too long to come home."

He went on to explain how Silva's father had destroyed his knee on his way to being a national football star and had never really recovered from the loss. I had heard such stories before. It was not uncommon really. After he hurt himself he didn't know who he was or what to do. Dreams can be too heavily invested in. So it appeared he had simply become a louse after the accident. He did nothing for the better part of five years, grew sedentary, and played the piano. The only thing in life he still loved was Silva, and so after his wife left him, he took Silva to Africa, where she had always wanted to go.

We stopped at a little bread shop and Camillo joked with the older woman behind the counter. I smiled and she spoke to me in Italian. Camillo translated: Where are you from?

"I am from Boston," I said a little too loud. She smiled and rattled off a short story of some kind. Camillo nodded, laughed with her and then we left with some baking ingredients for Carina.

On the way back we went slow because the rain was falling hard enough to crush the grass by the side of the road. Camillo concentrated on the road and I leaned back and tried not to worry about a head-on collision. So now I knew more than I wanted to. I knew where her father was. And I knew that someday she would go to look for him. It was inevitable, and for some reason I felt she had a role for me to play in her going. It made me nervous.

After we arrived back at the villa, Camillo and I walked in on a fight. It was Oliver and Silva in front of the main fireplace. She was yelling at him in Italian. They both looked over at us when we walked through the door to the great hall. Camillo, sensing the danger said, she does this periodically with him, and then swiftly departed while relieving me of the bag I was holding. They were silent for a moment during which I inappropriately recognized how sexy Silva looked when she was angry. She became calmly fierce like a bullfighter might.

"Philip," she said sweetly, and walked over quickly and stood in front of me. She grabbed my hand a little too hard.

Her body was tense.

"We are getting out of here for a while Philip," she said and started to walk me toward the door.

I was helpless against her when she was like this. She exuded power and control with her anger that I was simply unequal to. I looked back at Oliver and his eye caught mine.

Oliver with the calm intensity of his eye could hold me and Silva with the fierce intensity of her anger could pull me. I couldn't look away from him and the tired expression he wore. I was sure then that this thing that was happening, whatever it was, was not good for any of us, but especially me.

I let Silva drag me out into the rain after she threw open the door. I lost eye contact with Oliver as I ducked my head against the falling water. Silva and I stood for a long moment in the downpour like fools, looking at each other. She smiled, like I should be enjoying this. For the first time since my arrival I wished I were home in Westfall. She looked inside coldly back at Oliver who was still standing there as if he had seen this all before. Then she slammed the door and took out her key locking us out and him in.

I didn't know what was wrong, where we were going, or what had just happened, but I followed. Silva was mostly naked considering the weather and I felt bad about it. Within less than a minute she was soaked through. I followed next to her, my hand still caught in her iron grip. I didn't dare ask where; I just went, cold as hell, up the hill from the villa to the village. We walked through the narrow, stone-gray streets to a spot in town where all the houses looked out over the valley below. We went in an open archway built into the middle of a wall running along the street with a white wooden caduceus placed above it. I figured the place was where Camillo still saw local patients.

The door opened up onto a stone courtyard with a four story stone house set on the side of the hill. A strange looking old bearded man wrapped in a heavy brown blanket sat under a lean-to by a woodpile smoking a pipe in a wooden chair. He just watched us as we ran through the rain to the large wooden door of the house and then inside. He didn't even nod. His eyes were just blue slits beneath a wide brim hat.

When we got inside Silva's clothes were stuck to her body so she pulled her shirt off in front of me. She still wasn't talking. She stripped off her pants, fast, before I think she lost the nerve to do it. She stood there in her underwear by the cold fireplace, squinting at me. A part of me had been waiting for something like this: Silva making herself naked in front of me, for me. But something felt wrong about it all. The place felt crowded with invisible men, Oliver included. I chose to ignore them.

"Take off your clothes or you will catch your death," she said.

I did so, slowly.

Then Silva started a fire in matter of minutes. While I undressed I wanted to ask her what was going on. But I just stood and watched her instead, in her almost see-through underwear and me in mine. Her body was wet, her hair ragged. I looked down at myself. There was no comparison, my feet suddenly looked gargantuan next to hers. As she squatted down to play with the fire she looked like a child, perfectly at ease in her almost boyishly slim beauty.

"I will find you a robe," she said with her back to me. Then she walked away and headed up some stairs.

I went over to stand by the fire and took my soaked shirt, socks, and pants and hung them from the nails set in the mantle. I was stripped down to my underwear waiting by the heat. It all felt surprisingly good considering the situation. When she came back she held two long, white, hotel-thick robes. She looked less angry now as she put hers on. She handed mine to me. It had a hood. It didn't seem my style, a long ankle length royal looking garment with a hood.

"Wear this?" I said. "I'll look ridiculous."

"No you won't," she said, and came closer with not a hint of her earlier anger. "Put it on and I will make some hot tea for us to drink."

"Is everything okay with Oliver?" I asked.

"Sure, he's just a stubborn bastard that's all. But don't worry about it. He's going into the city to paint and he wants to leave us here together for a few days. He's like that you know. Just running off and abandoning people when it suits him."

"I know what you mean."

"Don't get me wrong, Philip, I am thrilled to spend the time alone with you, it's just that I will have to do some preparation for the wedding. So you will be on your own for some of the time. Is that okay?"

"Sure," I said, feeling a little annoyed at Oliver as well. I had flown across the Atlantic ocean to see him. It seemed like he could be a little more hospitable.

"Listen," Silva said from the kitchen. I heard a microwave turn on. "Don't take it personally, that's what I have had to learn to do, even though it makes me angry. He's an artist and that's what comes first for him."

I agreed with her. In a minute she came out with her two cups of instant tea in hand.

"Now lets sit by the fire, and act like to civilized non-artists. What do you say?"

I agreed again.

Later that night we ate a private dinner of roasted pheasant, potatoes, and sautéed spinach and garlic. The rain was still pouring down outside. I was wondering what Silva's hidden agenda was. I tried to get at it by making an offer. I told her if she was interested in visiting me in Westfall, then, of course, both she and Oli could come. I would ask my father, to be sure, when I got home, but I couldn't imagine him objecting. He had been making rumbling noises about the house being too big, about selling if the real estate market improved. I looked across the table at her.

"What shall we do about him?" she said.

"Who?" I said.

"Oliver."

She ignored what I had said, which was a thing I remembered she did when she didn't want to talk about something I had brought up. I always felt too stupid to bring the subject up again, as if her ignoring it had said everything she had to say about it.

"I don't know...what do you mean?"

"Let's make him sweat," she said. "You know? He's been driving me up the wall ever since you got here. I don't know what it is. He won't talk to me. He won't do the simple things I asked him to do. It's like he wants me to be angry with him."

"So what is this all about Silva? Really."

"I don't know?"

"Well, what was he was supposed to tell me?" I figured I would ask her this just so she had the cover of Oliver to make her comfortable with whatever she really wanted with me.

She looked at the candles for a moment. I reached across and took her hand.

"What is it. Tell me. I will understand."

She lifted her head and met my eyes. They seemed to say, no, I might not understand.

I leaned back into my chair slowly and let go of her hand.

"How about I tell you later, after a night's rest?"

"Okay," I said casually. "Actually, you don't have to tell me at all if you don't like. Some things are better left unsaid."

She seemed to take in the idea and stir it around a bit. There was a long pause in the rain outside seemed to become louder. I could be content not knowing what the trouble was all about. There were some secrets of my own I would hold in exchange for never knowing the truth she held.

Then she said, "I don't get it! Oliver just gets these things in his head, you know, and then they stick and he doesn't think to explain them."

"Like him vanishing after he went to school in New York," I said.

She looked at me and I saw it suddenly in her eyes. How much it had hurt her those years when he was gone.

"I'm sorry I never wrote you, Silva. I tried to."

She sat there across from me, her hands on the table. Then she reached across the table and covered my hand with hers. Her hair was down across her shoulders and the fire light made her face smooth as marble. She smiled and squeezed my hand.

Then, a moment later she was up and doing the dishes. But it seemed we now had a place to begin. I didn't find out until later that Oliver had written Silva only a few times during his three years of traveling, compared to the dozens and dozens of post cards he sent me. She had been so much more in the dark about his state of mind. She must have often thought him dead. I should have written her. I could have, and I shouldn't have been so small to blame his behavior on her.

I stayed at the house, in the village of Zagara that evening, while it continued to rain. Silva went back that night after dinner and gathered all my things from the villa for me and brought them over to the new house. She said it was better this way because some out of town relatives were coming to stay at the villa and needed my room. I was fine with being out the house that Angela had prophesized was no good for me. Plus with Oliver in the city now there was little reason to go back. The village of Zagara offered its own small twisting streets and visual delights and mysteries despite the rain and low clouds.

On her way out of the courtyard I saw Silva stop and talk to the old man sitting under the lean-to. She pointed at the house and he shook his head and then she left him to sit there by the wood and smoke. I wondered what it was about.

When Silva returned she made me comfortable, but she also made it clear that she didn't feel like talking about Oliver anymore, or anything that had happened back at the villa or what the trouble was really about.

So that night we both fell asleep on couches in front of the fire after talking for hours. It was a strange for me. She told me stories about the first summer after graduation when she was in Italy. The summer I had hoped they would both stay with me. She made it sound like a golden age when she and Oliver and some new Italian friends spent a month on the Adriatic coast in a small town. She rattled off names of people, Rafael, Benita, Salvatore, Angello, and Antonio. They were all lean legged soccer players, the whole bunch it seemed. Slowly a somewhat lurid tale, I felt, began to unravel, about the affairs each of them had while on the coast. It was her summer of romance, as she called it. I watched her all through the tale, through her stories of who was with whom, and who did what where. I don't know why she told it all to me.

Maybe to spite me for never writing her myself over the last three years. Whatever the reason, I took it all in calmly, but all I discovered of value was that the Antonio who had been her lover that summer, also happened to be the same man who was supposed to show me to the convent on my first day in Italy. It turned out he and Silva had been together for some time and Silva had cut it off with him before I came over. At least it explained his behavior. He must have been suspicious of me, the American friend coming over after Silva had broken up with him. Silva even admitted that Antonio was convinced I was her old American boyfriend come to claim her. And she said she was fine with that. That it had been off and on with him for three years and it never worked out. He is a playboy, she said.

    Silva woke me in the morning with a breakfast of buttered toast, eggs, and coffee. We had slept across from each other on our own couches in front of the fire. There was something marvelous about it that reminded me of the slow nights we had shared in my dorm room back in Westfall when Oliver had been in the infirmary and Silva sneaked in through the window to sleep curled up with me in bed. She said she couldn't sleep alone while Oliver was in such a bad state. I didn't argue.

    Over the next few days Silva created jobs for me. It took me a whole day to write out a long list of Italian names on each name card for the reception tables. My calligraphy was good, it was the only class I had taken with Silva in Westfall and so we both worked on the cards that first morning. Silva spent the afternoon back at the villa working with Carina on food preparations for the wedding while I finished the writing assignment.

That night we had another fine dinner alone and found ourselves drunk enough to dance around the kitchen with no music. There were a few moments when it felt like it used to be, nobody hurt, nobody hiding anything. Then she stepped away from me.

"Well...we can still do that well, can't we?"

"Yes," I said, just staring at her.

"Let's clean this place up and go sit by the fire," she said. We did, and then fell asleep on our couches again. But this time, in the middle of the night, she crawled onto my couch to sleep.

When I awoke the next morning she was gone, there was a note explaining she had errands to do. So I read a short book sitting on the coffee table written in five languages about the history of Zagara. I learned the town took its unusual name from a Greek doctor and alchemist who has been summoned by the Vatican in the 1600's because of his famous healing powers. Apparently the man never made it to Rome but died in the village after he reached it and discovered its population suffering from what modern doctors thought was some form of Cholera. In any event he had a moment of divine inspiration and somehow seemingly saved many of the villagers, and yet he himself died from the disease in the end. The village renamed itself after him, and over the centuries since then a legend grew up around Zagar. He became a sort of unofficial saint. Not because people where healed when they came to the village, but because Doctors, when they visited and sat in the courtyard outside where Zagar had worked, often received inspirations concerning unsolvable cases they were working on. This had been going on for centuries apparently, ever since the 1600's, and doctors from all over the world made a sort of pilgrimage to Zagara, some out of need and some perhaps out of respect.

I looked out the window to see the old man who's odd presence now made some sense, but he was gone already. Perhaps, he had found whatever cure he was looking for.

When Silva returned I told her how I had read about the unofficial Saint Zagar. She stood behind my chair for a moment and rubbed my shoulders and neck and said it was really quite amazing. Most of the people who came to visit she said, were European but some came from Egypt as well where they say Zagar had been trained. She said they usually all end up talking with Camillo for some time as well.

"Some of them stay here in this house when they visit," she said.

I mentioned that the book said that the most well known pilgrim to Zagara was the famous psychiatrist Dr. Carl Jung and that he had come here from Zurich and received a dream in which it is rumored that Zagar revealed to him a secret concerning the symbols of Alchemy. Silva laughed and said it must be true because a lot of the doctors who visit come from Switzerland, she said.

"That must make Zagar the unofficial Saint of dream interpretation," I said.

Silva agreed.

"Oliver would like that," I said.

She didn't say anything. Instead she kept rubbing my neck and shoulders too. I was surprised at how strong her hands were and told her so.

She said that she had taken a massage course in the city.

"Well, you are the only woman I know who does this hard enough," I said.

"Oh, really, and how many other woman have you been with?"

"Only just a few in my dorm freshman year and they were weak compared to you."

"Only a few? You're being modest. I am sure all the girls wanted a chance."

She came around the other side of the chair then and stood in front of me. I looked up at her.

She waited, smiled, then said, "Want some lunch?"

So this is how it was. We had quiet dinners, conversation flowed, and the next night, Silva and I slept in the same room, in the same bed. It was her idea. These couches are ruining my back she said, and then took my hand and led me upstairs. We talked at night like best friends do, until we both fell asleep. I woke up in the middle of the last of our perfect nights and just looked over to see she was still there, a soft bundle of blankets and breath.

The evening before the wedding I decided I needed to get out for a long walk. Before I went, I asked Silva over dinner about the wedding guests. She said all her "friends" would be there. The bride's side needed more representation. Oliver and I were to stand on her side of the church along with the soccer players. Silva had to stand on the groom's side because this was her third cousin getting married. It was going to happen in the small chapel that sat opposite the entrance to the villa driveway. It was built by Silva's family and everyone from the surrounding area who was related to the family was married there. The whole thing made me feel like an outsider and she could tell. She said it would be a beautiful wedding and that this couple had real love between them. I liked the way she said it, real love. Like she understood it the way I did. That made me feel better, especially the way she looked at me when she said it. It balanced out the thought of meeting her libidinous friends. So I went for my walk after our dinner.

I headed out with my boots on. As I walked, whatever doubts still dogged me about the entire situation between Oliver and Silva, whatever it was about, found me little impressed.

It had begun to rain when I stumbled upon him. Oliver was walking in the vineyards along the roadside. Silva hadn't told me he was back from the city. I contemplated avoiding him, but then decided I should talk to him while I had this easy chance. I had things I should and still needed to tell him. And there was Silva and myself too, getting closer than I ever imagined we would. It was not right to leave him in the dark about such things. I waited a few minutes until he closed the distance and then I made it like I was just coming off a path from the other direction. I fell in and walked beside him. He barely noticed me, and it seemed he was in a bad mood. I decided to wait it out. We were silent as I fell into his rhythm. We weaved our way along on a path over bumps and ruts in the trail along-side the road. We followed the path past the small family chapel, then we stopped under a line of pines planted long ago at the edge of the road. I was beginning to wish I hadn't joined him. The silence was uncomfortable. I looked up into the cavernous dripping branches and felt the darkening sky above.

"How are you?" I said too loudly. He stopped in the middle of the road.

I looked at him and then at the muddy earth, and at his long hands hanging. They looked blue. He saw me notice his hands.

"Bad circulation," he said.

His face was pale and his lips were also a little bluish. He held up his hands. We looked at them together, me in disbelief.

"What are you doing out here?"

He breathed heavy and warm into them. Then I reached out and closed his fingers into fists and covered them with my hands.

For the first time I felt okay about touching him. It was because of Silva, I knew. Something about knowing she was out there thinking of me gave me confidence with Oliver. I would tell him about she and I.

"You need to make heat," I said. I wrapped my hands over his fists and tightened down. We stood for a while waiting, facing each other. His hands were still cold.

"Let's go back, you're freezing from the rain. You'll catch your death out here," I said.

"You sound like Silva," he said.

"It's true."

"No, it's not. I caught my death a long time ago." He looked down the road.

"What are you talking about."

"Nothing Philip, forget it."

"When did you get back from the city?"

"What?"

"The city."

"I wasn't in the city," he said.

"But, Silva said...."

Suddenly he laughed and tilted his head back. "Is that what told you?"

He said Silva had fooled him, too. She told him I had caught a cold from the rain when we ran away and that I was insisting on staying quarantined so that no one else would suffer.

"I'm fine," I said.

Then we stood there for a while feeling bamboozled. He looked a little less pale and blue than before. Then I thought maybe Silva had lied to each of us just so she could have some time alone with me and thus finally begin cementing what we began at Westfall years ago. The thought gave me courage.

"Oli, Silva and I are getting along rather well. I hope, well, you don't mind."

He frowned back at me as the seemingly unpleasant realization spread through him.

"Okay, I'm sorry, but it just happened, you see?"

"It's not that Philip!" he said bluntly, almost mean.

I was stunned for a moment.

"What the hell are you so upset about, Oli?"

"You think this is all about you, Philip. But you don't see beyond yourself. You live here," and he pointed to the temple next to his destroyed eye.

I took a step back from him but he suddenly grabbed my hands and wouldn't let them go. I looked into his one good eye. It was dark all around us. Suddenly the raincoat I had borrowed felt very heavy, and I wanted to get back to the house and climb into bed with Silva. The pine trees above whispered and shook in the wind. He had pointed to his eye.

Then I saw it all. They both knew. I had been right. This was all an elaborate set up of some kind.

They both knew I was the one who had wounded him that day. He was just waiting for me to tell him the truth. Well I wasn't going to do it. Not then, like that, knowing he already knew and had held that back for years. I tried to shake my hands free.

"Let go, Oli you bastard!" But he wouldn't, he had snaked his hands up to my wrists and meant to hold on.

"Let go. What do you want from me?"

"Look at me, Philip. Look at me for once. What do you see?" I refused to look. It was all I could take.

I threw myself at him, my whole body in an attempt to get him to let go, but I slipped in the mud and we both tumbled to the ground. He still didn't let go.

I am not exactly sure what happened next because it happened fast. We were rolling on the ground. I was larger than he by then, stronger too. In fact he seemed frail as we struggled, weaker than I ever imagined he could be. But I was in a long rain coat and couldn't seem to get unwrapped from the hideous thing as it got caught in my legs and kept me from getting up. The mud splattered in my face and I spit it out. I tried to push him away but after a moment I was just trying to fight him. Just this once, to win against him. Then I was rolling down over the embankment alone and he was gone.

He had released me.

It took me a moment to recover. Then I saw him running away. I wanted to catch him. To take the bastard down. I wasn't going to let him run away from this. I felt I had an advantage now. So I chased.

He went around a bend and out from under the cover of the pines and into ominous looking gray drizzle. I tried to run harder. I splashed through puddles, mud, water, rocks beneath my boots, the air coming in cold gulps, but still Oliver sped ahead around a bend. A moment later I was there at that same place but he was at the next, always at the next, and then, I couldn't see him at all. I went down into a gully, up a rise, down again, then level with the sky above, then falling down, water, mud, darkness.

I was stepping on the damn coat. It got tangled in my legs like a small dog. Mud and water hit my face, hands, legs, and his footsteps were sounding off in the distance. I could hear them, lighter than any man can run in mud, and then gone. He wasn't looking back. Wasn't making sure I was there. He wasn't waiting for me.

I was up on all fours, my hands in the mud, but I didn't care. I tried to rise but my own feet betrayed me and caught me up in the folds of the jacket and sent me down in the mud on my side. I rolled onto my back and let my eyes close. The rain fell slowly on my eyelids, cheeks and neck.

Lying there, I remembered that day in Westfall when Oliver had taken the dictionary, and how he had looked into my eyes, and declared that I couldn't see, and then, as he walked away with the dictionary, he asked if I was deaf. Maybe he was right. Maybe I never saw anything as it was, not him, not Silva, not myself. Maybe my truth, how I remembered everything, my whole life, my mother's death, maybe it was just a story I told myself, a lie.

    I felt my heart slow and then felt the cold seep through the raincoat. The sweat I was making was going cold too fast and I knew this was how I would truly get sick. The cold began to rise and sink in my back, a battle between warm flesh and cold earth. Rainwater made trails over me to find its way to the ground, only to surround me in pools. What was Silva doing to me? We had something, we were making something, and now? What the hell was I doing here, with these insane people I didn't know and had never really known? I should have been at home with my friends from college, my real friends--loyal friends.

    I passed through shivering and onto numb quickly. I was comfortable there. I didn't care about Oliver anymore, or if he ever knew it was I who had hurt him that day. I didn't want him to come back for me. I didn't care if he never slowed down for me.

Δ   Δ   Δ

    It was the day of my graduation from Westfall Academy. I was having "the big party" after the event. Someone told me it was going to rain. I was worried. People were coming over, most of whom I didn't know well. We were going to barbecue outside. When the first drops began to fall, Oliver was out lighting the fire pit and altogether ignored the storm as if he couldn't hear the thunder. I let him go ahead and do it and, incredibly, he had the pit roaring with flames before the storm hit.

I watched Oliver to make sure he didn't catch himself on fire. He backed away from the flames, onto the porch, where he began to sketch the fire in his book, content to watch it and not play with it. We were waiting for our first guests to arrive.

The party began slowly then exploded in numbers as most of the senior class walked over from school with their parents. Then the parents left and some of the students with them. With a solid forty students we entered and then rolled on into an all-night stretch. The storm passed over us in what took about four hours of continual thunder that started around eight: lightning, light rain, hard rain, then light rain again, and then wind. I was paying close attention for it was the best lightning storm in years. The party mostly ignored it and ranged all over the house. I danced once with Teresa, who kept leaning her head on my shoulder, kissing my ear and embarrassing me with her affections. Some of the other guys were giving me that look I had grown accustomed to, a sort of odd mix of envy and respect, as if just because Teresa had a crush on me I might know something they didn't. Well, perhaps I did. But if so, I didn't know how to use it.

As a lightning addict, I stayed away from the dance floor during most of the best part of the storm once it began. It allowed other people to dance with Teresa, and me a chance to find Silva and have this whole Italy thing out with her. Oliver, it seemed had vanished. I had no idea where he was for most of the party. But it was typical. I was sure he wanted to just escape and watch, listen, and maybe find one person he could talk to all night long. I just hoped he had already spoken with Silva about our new summer plan.

Silva, of course, was the one really in charge. Everyone asked her where things were. I believe they thought it was her house, and for one night, it was.

I heard her explaining her plans about going to Italy. She was excited, and those who listened were excited for her. They were in the kitchen with half a dozen other people, talking and drinking and such. It was she and Greg. He had trapped her between the phone and the stove, people on both sides of them. I pretended to get something out of the fridge, to see if she needed saving from someone. That's when I heard her say it. I was hidden behind three students who blocked her view of me so she didn't know I was there.

"Oliver and I are leaving in a few days. I bought the plane tickets weeks ago."

"How did you manage it?" Someone asked.

"Teresa put the tickets on her mother's credit card until I could pay her. I sold my harp today so that won't be a problem."

"That's great." Someone else said.

I was looking into a shelf of the refrigerator full of my father's salad dressings and mustards. After I was done looking for nothing I quickly left. I had to find Oliver. I hadn't known she already had the tickets, that Teresa had helped her. It was already a done deal. She had lied to me. I looked everywhere, and all the while I was planning, scheming some way in which I could alter the course of the near future. Silva just had the gift of making things happen her way. I was no match for her, but I still had to try.

It wasn't just because I would miss him when he was gone. I couldn't let Oliver go away not knowing the truth about who was really responsible for wounding him that day, at least, that is what I told myself.

    I was in the entry hall on my way to the cupola when she grabbed me--Teresa. I don't know how, but she had managed to get drunk in the half-hour since I had last seen her.

    "What are you doing, Philip?" she lisped.

    I was standing by the coat closet when she came at me. The door was open and I looked around for help, but they were all in league with her. She walked right up to me, placed her hands on my chest and ushered me back into the deep closet with her.

    "Teresa...I am looking for Oliver," I said as she held me and moved me straight back.

    "Maybe he's in the closet," she said and pushed me harder.

    "I don't think so..." The door closed behind her.

    She grabbed onto my shirt.

    "Teresa, I really can't. I'm the host."

    But then she had her hands in my hair and she was kissing me like it was the end of the world. I did nothing, at first. But it was impossible to detach myself from her. She held me for minutes and eventually she had her hands under my shirt. I gave in and let her do what it was she had apparently wanted to do for a long time. I rubbed my hands on her back and found myself thinking about what she might know of Silva and Oliver leaving. So I broke up her seduction with a question.

    "You helped Silva buy those plane tickets, didn't you?"

"Oh, I tried to stop her...such a beautiful harp," she said and kissed me again. It wasn't clear to me at all what had happened. Had she not bought the plane tickets? I wondered if Silva had been lying in the kitchen. Teresa wasn't making a lot of sense and she was in no mood to talk about Silva. I was starting to have a hard time breathing in the closet. Her perfume, her hands, the heat.

"We can't stay in here forever," I said finally.

"That's right. You're the host. And you need to find Oliver, don't you?" she said dropping her forehead to my chest. Her hair smelled of cigarettes.

"Yes," I said to her, "that's right."

She decided to leave me then.

"Okay Philip, if I can't have you for myself, then I will leave you alone. The way you like it."

For her anyway, it seemed a long chapter I was unaware of was over. Her plan: She would leave the closet first and then I should wait a minute as punishment for being coy for so long, and then for denying her in the end. Plus, she said, "I don't want everyone to see us together in here."

She apparently had other back up plans for the rest of the night.

I stood in the closet for more than a minute. The door was open a crack and I could breath deeply again. I slid to the floor and sat leaning against the wall. I listened to the party outside and with her gone I suddenly felt safe. It was good to be alone.

After some time I opened the closet door slowly and peeked out. No one was there. No one was dancing and no one was in the living room. I had the absurd feeling that the entire thing had been a joke: the party, Teresa, Oliver, Silva, and even my father. That they all had arranged this colossal deception to make me feel stupid. I couldn't hear anything except the storm. They had left. I wondered if perhaps I had been in the closet longer than I suspected. I walked out in the room and that's when I heard it. Thunder cracked over the house like a bomb. Then a great roar went up from the back porch. I peered around into the kitchen. No one there either. Through the kitchen I went to the den and around the corner. There they were all out on the back porch, storm-watching. The lights on the porch were off so they were all just a mass of shadows to me. I walked into the den and up to the closed sliding glass door. All the talking and laughing went silent when the next lightning flash came. For an instant, I saw them all, all of Teresa's and Silva's crowd, all the ones who lived at the center of things. There, too, was Oliver, standing farthest away by the porch railing. Teresa was hanging on one of Oliver's arms and Silva the other, and my father, right behind them all, a head taller than the rest. I saw the whole thing in a flash, before the crash of thunder smashed down.

Then, I turned away.

I went up the stairs, down the hall, and up to the cupola. It was there, high up, that I had always liked to be when I watched the storms. It was where my mother used to bring me. It was with her that I lost my fear of thunder as a child. Oliver and I, too, had been up to watch storms a few times together. We would lie on our backs and look up through the windows at the wild display.

So that's what I did. I ran away. A few times, I could hear them all below. I wanted to go down there, to be a part of things.

But I stayed, stuck between the desire to go down and join the human race and the need to stay, it seemed, forever up in the cupola.

Then, the need to decide was taken from me, he was there with me. I didn't even hear him. He was capable, just like Silva, of a seemingly preternatural. I wondered if this ability had something to do with the household they grew up in.

"I saw you at the sliding door," he said.

"How could you?"

"The same moment you saw us." There was a convenient silence in which we paused for thunder.

"I knew you wouldn't come out," he said and lay down next to me.

I kept silent for a while more. I had nothing to say to him.

"But I wish you had Philip. I wish you had."

"Me too," I said softly.

"I love this," he said speaking about the storm that was all around us.

"Yes, I know. But it won't last much longer."

"Oliver?" I said.

"Yes."

I don't know how much time passed but Oliver waited patiently for me to go on. I wanted to tell him about Silva and the tickets, about how she might have lied and betrayed us both. I wanted to tell him more too, more about everything, like how I had been the one who had hurt him that day, and how on the night before the accident, the night Silva first came to visit our dorm room that it had felt like he wanted to steal the memories of my mother from me. As if he wanted to take away the only thing I had left of her, use them all up for his art and then erase them later. And I wanted to tell him that I didn't think that it was an accident that day at the cook out. That I knew it wasn't. I had wanted to hurt him, just a little... so as to make him like the of rest of us, like Silva and myself, wounded.

I don't know how long it was before I gave up on myself, and he finally gave up on me. It was too much to say at once, to much for one breath. I didn't know how to confess.

"I'm sorry, Philip," he said.

"For what?" I said. Outside, the storm was angry and hissing wind against the window.

"I have a confession to make."

He was going to tell me something I didn't want to hear. I could feel it, so I said it first.

"You're going to Italy."

"No."

"You're not?"

"I don't know yet. But that wasn't what I was going to tell you."

"Are you going or not?"

"Well, yes, I'm going at some point. I can't let her go alone can I?"

"I knew it."

"We can work all that out, Philip. I will go after July fourth maybe. It's no big deal. But there is something else, more important," he said.

"What do you mean? What else is there? She's your stepsister. I don't have that so I can't say I really understand can I."

He ignored me and went on with his confession.

"On those nights, Philip? When we weren't painting? I wasn't in the closet."

No great crash of thunder followed no lightning to accompany it, the revelation. If anything, just a lull in the battle outside and the sad, faded pattering of rain on the aluminum roof. He went on but I won't repeat it. It was the only time I ever heard Oliver back away, rationalize and try to heal some perceived error on his part. For me, I wouldn't understand what he was saying to me for some time, and wouldn't understand it all, exactly, the full implications that is, until that night of the wedding in Italy, three years later.

I said sharply, "Well, you could have just told me you were sneaking around in the dark. You didn't need to protect me from anything. I mean you broke a hundred rules this year, what was the big deal?"

"I'm sorry. I just thought there were some things we should both tell each other."

"Well I would rather you hadn't. For God's sake it made me feel safe thinking you were in that closet."

"I'm sorry," he said again.

"You know, it's not like I'm not capable of being alone. I've been that way before." I sat up suddenly. "Jesus Oli, why couldn't you have just let me believe you where there all along and left it alone? You know, you should learn to live with your guilt and not pass it around."

For once I was right and had won the impossible, an argument with Oliver. But the stupid irony of my victory was crushing me. Who after all, knew more about betrayal than myself?

I stood up then and left. I went down the dark cupola stairs quickly, trying to keep the vision of his eye out of my mind. Then past my father's bedroom. I thought how in the end all we ever are is alone, and Oliver had proved it for me. Things are never how they appear, never turn out how you want unless you lie to make things happen your way. That was Silva, and that was Oliver, and maybe that was me. But if anything, they had done worse. I had trusted them and they had betrayed me. They both probably knew about selling the harp and going to Italy, they just didn't think I was strong enough to take it. They were wrong. I had been abandoned before by far better and I had gotten back up and kept walking, and I had never burdened anyone with it after. At least I had the strength to keep what was mine to myself, where it belonged.

The grandfather clock in the hall chimed in about that time. I was on my way to the kitchen. It was two a.m. The party was over, everyone was gone. Silva had taken care of everything, even cleaned up and left a note. I didn't read it. I didn't care. I felt like a fool. Even more so when I realized, somewhere in the back of my mind, that I had just missed the easiest chance I would ever have to confess to him the truth about being the one who destroyed his eye.

I put my hands on the porcelain sink and leaned in. What did it matter if he ever knew the truth? "I just don't care anymore," I said to the sink.

"About what?" Silva said. I turned around too quickly.

Silva stepped back a little.

"Philip?"

"You knew all along Silva. No need to lie anymore."

"I'm sorry Philip. He told you didn't he?"

"Yes, he did."

"I should have told you, I'm sorry."

"It would have been the polite thing to do. I mean...I can't believe you had plane tickets already and you knew that you were going to sell the harp, and taking him with you, too.

"Philip, what are you talking about?"

I stood up straight and took a step toward her. I had the uneasy feeling I was about to strike her.

"Don't try and lie your way out now. I'm not blind like your stupid brother."

She took a step back from me. The outside flood light spread a thin gray gauze through the kitchen window and across her face. I couldn't read her expression, but I could feel it like heat. She was already backing away, out the kitchen door, and then she was gone.

I just let her go.

I heard the front door close, not loud, not soft, just an empty sound. I turned back to the sink and fell onto my elbows, leaning over to hug myself.

Δ   Δ   Δ

"Philip, wake up!" Silva said.

She brought herself down close to me, laid her hand on my cheek, laid her body down on mine like living fire and kissed me. I knew it was she, the touch of her perfect fingers making perfect sounds come alive in my body. There were tears in her eyes. Maybe she thought I had been hit by a car, had almost died. It didn't matter to me.

I don't know how she knew to find me out on that road, but she did and I loved her for it, for not abandoning me.  "Philip, what happened to you, you look terrible. Are you hurt."

I simply looked up at her and smiled. I was still glad to see her.

"Come on, we need to get you back to the house and in a bath, you're freezing."

She helped me up and we walked up the hill together to the village house. Then she lead me up stairs to the bathroom where she started filling the tub with hot water. Her hands were kind as she undressed me. Naked, I was not so muddy, but she insisted I bathe and get warm. Once she had me in the water, and was confident I was indeed not injured, she left to make me some tea. When she returned she set the tea next to the tub to cool a bit. Then she knelt behind me with a pitcher and soap and began to wash the earth from my hair, her fingers and the trickles of water sending delicious jolts of warmth through my shoulders. She told me of the wedding preparations, and about how well things would go tomorrow. She didn't even ask again how I had ended up in my condition on the road. I loved her for this too.

After the bath she tucked me in the large double bed. She lit a fire in the fireplace. My last image before I drifted off to sleep was of Silva undressing. I tried to stay awake but couldn't. I hadn't known I was so tired. I drifted and dreamed of cats, chapels, and menacing blue trees. I must have slept for only a few minutes for when I awoke she was there in the bed with me, her legs cold as they tangled, rubbed, and burrowed with mine, trying to absorb my warmth. She made quiet noises of achieving comfort that made me want to pull her close into me, tighter than we already were. We stayed tight for minutes, while her breathing became deeper, soft, and I wished to say something, ask questions about love, but I couldn't break the silence. Moonlight was coming though the window. I realized the clouds must be leaving and that the wedding would have a fine day. Then she pressed her face closer to mine.

I could just see her eyes in the half light of the fire. I was surprised to find them sad. But then she was kissing me, a pressing, sucking softness that tugged deep inside at my heart. When she climbed on top of me, I held her thin hips and then ran my hands as far down as they would reach and then up her naked body, over her legs, strong back, smooth neck, and into the sweet smell of her soft curls. Her mouth moved softly. She pressed herself against me, started a rocking movement of fleeting pressures against my pelvis, like a hesitant butterfly above water. I watched and felt her change above me. Slowly her breathing came faster, then she found me and lowered herself in one terrible slow soft pour of motion.

It was I who was up early the next morning, making coffee and going out to find her favorite pastries at the shop down the alley. There was a rare clarity in that blue morning sky, crisp as November air in Westfall. I walked through the streets and cats of various colors watched me pass by.

I returned and woke Silva. She smiled up at me, like a child awaking from a child's good dream. I could do this forever I thought, and kissed her on the forehead. We had an easy and simple breakfast together there on the bed and then we made love again and thoughts of Oliver were far from my mind. Then she said she had to go, and that I should come to the wedding at ten. I said I would be there.

She washed and dressed while I watched her and she didn't mind me watching. Then, after she left, I gathered my things. We were heading back to the city the next morning. I had three days before my flight left and the time now seemed too short. As I dressed I pulled the shark's tooth from my other pants and decided to bring it with me to the wedding. Maybe I would give it back to Oliver. Maybe I was done with him at last.

It took me a short ten minutes to walk to the church. It was a fine walk. All I could do was think about Silva. I just wanted the wedding and the day to be over so I could be alone with her again. I arrived early and found Oliver waiting for me. He took my arm and we walked down the aisle to our seat without any recognition of what had occurred the night before. I thought it was odd, both taking my arm and ignoring the obvious, which was something both he and Silva shared in terms of social custom.

We moved in to find our seats and sat down without a word.

Oliver looked excellent, his linens were pressed and he wore a simple but elegant patch with a red triangle on it. After a few minutes I saw Silva come in with another woman. She looked like Silva, just not as beautiful. Silva saw me and winked. All was going well. Just when it seemed everyone was in I saw him. Antonio, with clothes much finer than mine, was sliding past people to end up sitting right next to Silva. He was just arrogant enough to show up late. Then the music started.

I tried to keep my mind on the ceremony. It was long. After a while I forgot about Oliver and Antonio and instead wondered what my wedding would look like, say, with Silva. It would have to be here in this church, I decided. Then she would come back to the States. Oliver might go back down to school in New York, it was about time, and she could take classes at Boston College. I could see it. It was plausible. Then the ceremony was over and I was brought back to the chapel, my fantasies vanishing as we made our way out.

I managed to meet Silva in the aisle and offered her my arm, she took it and we walked out together. I thought I saw a jealous glance from Antonio, but I resisted looking behind me to be sure. Outside the chapel, on the stone steps, all was cordial and sweet. Antonio had come out holding Oliver's arm. It was then, that I discovered that Antonio could speak perfect English.

"You look fine Philip, for an American."

"Not so bad yourself, for a greyhound."

"Excuse me," he said. "I am not so familiar with that term."

Silva looked at me with a *be careful* eye. Oliver was already wearing a smirk.

"It's a euphemism for one who comes in late for a wedding," I said.

His response was something in Italian, and a short laugh.

"Yes, I was bad to be such a dog," he said. "But I could not find where Silva hid my necktie," he said smiling at me.

"Lets get on our way," Silva said and quickly grabbed my arm and started down the steps. Oliver raised his eyebrows in answer to my silent question to weather that last Antonio comment had any merit at all.

Silva and I ignored everyone as we walked down the drive to the villa. Every so often she spoke to someone in Italian, but mostly we looked around us at the splendid grounds, and the light streaming down. Off to the left were three white horses, I asked if it was some tradition. Silva just nodded. A huge bull named Brutus was off to our right separated from the horses by the drive and the two stone walls on each side. He stood like a huge statue in the tall grass, in perfect stillness, his nose lifted high and head turned to see us better, as we, and the entire procession, walked past him. I heard some young man, last to pass by him, yell out his name loudly, cajoling him into a bellow, loud as a ship's horn it seemed.

Inside we began to drink immediately.

The tables were covered with white linen table cloths, flowers, and hundreds of candles. Even in the morning with the huge double doors open, the hall could be dark and cold. But on this day it looked brilliant. Crystal glasses and wine bottles were on every table. I found my seating name card had been placed at a table with Oliver, Salvatore, Benita, Angello, and Rafael. I was a little confused. I looked around. Silva's card was not on the table. I turned around to tell her there had been some mistake, but she was gone. She had wandered over to another table to talk to someone I didn't recognize. It was another young man, maybe a cousin I thought. She gave him a hug and they kissed cheeks as they all did. Then she kissed him on the lips. And that's how it all began. From that moment on I felt myself and my world starting to slip away. I stood with Oliver and Benita who were talking about something I wasn't interested in. Oliver introduced her to me and after that moment my eyes followed Silva all over the room. I tried not to be obvious about it.

"Philip, Silva says, you're from Boston?" I turned to see that Oliver had left me alone with Benita.

"Well..."

"What is Boston?" Benita's voice was beautiful. Her pronunciation of the English words was unsure and elegant at the same time.

"A city."

"I see," she said, not quite understanding. "Would you like to get us some liquor?"

So we went over to the bar and from there Benita found someone else to talk to. I got my first rum and coke and managed, with a drink in my hand, to stand aside and observe. I watched and watched, Silva move. She knew how to work a room. But what bothered me wasn't her social grace and my lack of it. I had always known she had this gift. It was the way she engaged with all these soccer player types. They all reminded me of Greg, Silva's one time sort of boyfriend back in Westfall.

"He has great legs," is what she once told me about him. I remember I had checked them out in the locker room once after cross-country practice when the soccer players came in. I couldn't see the big deal but I tried to get a good sense of them none the less. Then I checked my own out in the full length mirror on the wall by the coaches' office.

"You have wonderful eyes," was a thing she might have said to me, might as well have said, because Silva always looked at eyes. That, at least we had in common. And we both knew I had the most wonderful eyes of all. It was true. I knew that. They were my mother's eyes. I had done some objective studies. I became like a woman, noticing the color of eyes wherever I went. Antonio, the leach, he had crap for eyes as far as I was concerned, a sort of muddy brown with absolutely no light in them.

I finished my drink and had another. These were the things I was thinking as Silva worked the room. That maybe she had shared a night with every one of these soccer players she moved among. The summer of romance sounded like a summer of debauchery to me.

Oliver had vanished with Salvatore. They looked fairly deep in conversation the last time I looked over, and then they were gone. Salvatore, Silva had told me a few nights before, was a soccer player musician who wanted to be a painter. He and Oliver were close, is what she said.

I saw my moment for action from a distance. I had been standing alone for too long. I knew this. Silva was giving all these men hugs and kisses. Then, I saw her drink was empty. So I ordered her another and the bartender remembered what she was having when I pointed to her. She was talking to an older couple when I came upon her. I tried to smooth my way in and offered her the drink. The grandparents of the bride didn't speak any English, so there was a few brief moments of translation on Silva's part, she was fluent in Italian after three years. Then something went wrong. They continued to talk and something Silva had said had caused concern to appear in their faces. She tried to explain in more depth but I could see it wasn't working and they were looking at me with a sort of disdain.

"Silva, what is it?"

"Never mind, it doesn't matter. They have been listening to Antonio."

I couldn't believe this. Antonio was running a campaign against me.

"Silva, about Antonio. I wanted to talk to you about that necktie thing he said earlier."

"Oh, don't worry Philip, he is just jealous is all. But later, lets talk, okay," she said looking partly serious. Then she smiled.
"I have to mingle now, okay, its part of the job here for me." She said and then kissed me on the mouth. I felt much better.

But, none-the-less I decided to retreat after she went back into her job. I went back to the bar again where I had another drink and stayed out of everyone's way. A half-hour later we were all eating and Benita was on my right, Oliver on my left. Benita was already drunk and had begun to come on to me in an uncomfortable way. She kept putting her hand on my leg when she wanted to talk to me. I could see Silva at a table not far away, and I had been surprised and resentful to see Antonio sit down next to her when the meal began. The bastard, he must have fixed it somehow, switched our cards. I watched him like a hawk throughout the meal. He whispered to her once, twice, and then put his arm around the back of her chair while he smoked his cigarette. But I couldn't watch him all the time because Benita was getting after me. I was so distracted by the entire situation that I couldn't enjoy the food, and I don't even remember what Carina prepared. By the end of the meal Benita was speaking to me in Italian and Angello, who was next to her, was laughing at her, as she fawned. I tried to evade her by getting up to leave but she was drunk and leaning on me. I decided after the meal I would ask Silva to dance out on the patio where the band was playing and ditch Benita in the process. I didn't understand why Silva hadn't told Benita to stay away from me.

    We had been sitting for almost an hour and a few times Silva had gotten up and circulated through the tables. She even visited our table and talked with all her soccer players. When she got to me she leaned over and I could smell the alcohol and perfume mixing like ambrosia in her hair. I closed my eyes just to smell it.

    "So, what do you think of my soccer players," she says to me.

    "Nice, very nice. But you are nicer."

    "Aren't you sweet...I think Benita is in love with you."

    "I thought you said she had a boyfriend."

    "She does, Rafael, he's right across from you. He likes you too."

    "What? Silva, I feel–"

    "Don't worry, I'll fix everything." She stood up and began to walk around the table. I tried to stop her but she evaded my grasp and I bent my head and put it in my hands as she whispered seductively into Rafael's ear. He laughed and said something back into hers. Then he turned to me and lifting his glass said something in Italian which Benita and Angello and Silva all laughed at.

Salvatore and Oliver were deep in conversation again. I was embarrassed but raised my glass anyway. I proceeded to say something in English which no one understood, not even me, and we toasted again in a sort of half hearted way. Silva stayed talking with Rafael for a few minutes and Benita went over to join them. I sat there alone like an old dog not sure what had just happened. Then, Silva just left. She never came back to me or even looked my way.

She and Rafael and Benita went away, toward the kitchen and I was at the table alone, with Oliver and Salvatore talking away. I decided that was enough. I got up and wandered through the small crowds of talking folks who were all up out of their chairs by this time. I went past the fireplace and up the stairs to Silva's room. I thought I might just get away for a minute and try to get myself together.

The bed, the chairs, and the desk were all covered with coats. I felt like lying down on the bed and never waking up. Parties were bad enough, but in a foreign country I was just altogether unfit for them.

On the windowsill I found the rest of Oliver's bottle of rum. I picked it up. Just a little less than half the bottle was left. Then, through the window, I heard the music change and saw the dancing begin. I watched them go through the wedding dance rituals. After a while everyone was dancing and I knew I had to get down there.

I could imagine it, Antonio dancing with Silva. The very thought sent fire up my back. I tried to spot her down there but couldn't see her yet. I decided what I needed was a little spirit to get me going. I was the most sober person out of Silva and her friends, and I decided that was the problem. So I drank the rest of the rum without stopping, in exactly eleven swallows. I wiped my lips and put the top back on the bottle. Now I felt full, ready to go. I decided to move quickly and use the benefits of the rum before I lost my nerve.

Then, I heard someone shuffle behind me. I turned to see the black little rumpled form of Angela standing there in the doorway. Predictably, she had her rolled up umbrella-bat in hand. She looked at me. Then she looked at the bottle I had just drained and still held in my hand. She nodded her head, tapped her umbrella on the floor, muttered something to herself in Italian and walked away. For her, the prophecy about me and this house was obviously well on its way to being confirmed. Maybe she was right, but at that point I didn't care anymore. If events were destined to turn out badly for me, as she predicted, then what choice did I have. I might as well take my best shot, I thought.

In the kitchen, I found her. Silva was sitting on the big table. Antonio was standing right next to her and the others were around the table, too. They were laughing loudly before I came in, so I paused until normal conversation had resumed. Even I knew one should never walk into the middle of a great laugh. But I hadn't paused long before a suspicion that they were laughing about me began to creep into my mind. I went around the corner and Benita yelled out my name loudly, she was even more drunk than before, but happy to see me. I, as yet, was feeling nothing from the rum, but I knew it was there so I didn't hesitate.

"Silva," I said, after walking right up in front of her and Antonio.

"I think someone out there on the patio wants us to dance." The sweetest smile I had ever seen greeted me. Then I looked at Antonio and I saw it in his crap brown eyes, my victory.

I held out my hand and she slipped off the table and landed on the floor with a double click of heels. She was wearing a tight black dress, and she pulled it down a little before we left.

I believe they all followed us out to the patio.

I felt like I had never danced better in my entire life. And Silva too. I was sure people would recognize how well we could dance together and thus conclude that we were meant to be. By that time I had forgotten about all the rum I had consumed and I suspect that I deserved to collapse on the dance floor, but there were a few minutes, precious, seemingly outside of time itself, when we did not bump into anyone and we created the most perfect of patterns, ones that mended my internal frustrations.

The bliss didn't last long. Before we were far into the next waltz Antonio and Benita cut in. Benita took me out of Silva's hands and Antonio took Silva. What could I do? Hit him? I should have perhaps, right then. But there is certain etiquette, there are rules, and battles on the dance floor have their special means of victory. That is what I told myself at the time anyway. Benita and I had ten, maybe twenty steps of slightly less perfection than Silva and I, and then it was over. She sensed something was wrong with me and took me to sit down on a bench that had been set up for people like myself who could not longer walk or see straight. We sat together and she spoke to me but it made very little sense. I wasn't listening anyway. I was watching Antonio, with his hand low on Silva's back, as they danced slowly. I decided I was going to cut in before that hand went any lower. I never made it.

    I didn't wake up for hours. When I did, I was still drunk and I had a bump on my head. It was late in the night, long after twelve, the moon was low and full, ready to set, maybe two hours till dawn. I was still feeling sick from the alcohol, and all my senses were impaired. Yet I picked right up where I remembered having left off, angry.

    I was in an empty bathtub wrapped in a blanket without my shirt. I didn't know how I had gotten there. I tried to look at myself but it was dark in the tub and the rest of the bathroom and my eyes felt somehow less capable, as if filled with tears. I was too tired, too sick in my head, stomach, and toes to look for a light. But I remembered a cartoon I had seen once in which some sort of animal was in a stupor and stuck his head under water in order to wake up and clear his head. So I searched for the spray gun and found it, confident I now knew its correct use after days of successful baths up at the house in Zagara. Then I leaned over so as not to get my pants all wet and turned on the water. The villa made growling sounds and the water came out in fast bursts until it hit me on the neck and made me real back from the cold. I groped for the other knob and eventually, after what seemed like hours of adjustment, I had a good mixture of hot and cold and I put the thing over my head. The odd pounding sound that had been churning away in my head increased. But I relaxed as the wetness brought me back to life.

I lifted my hand and felt for the bump on my forehead. It hurt.

I got up, slowly, made my way out of the tub to the sink, lights on, and looked in the mirror.

I looked around the bathroom and saw it was in complete disarray. At the time I imagined that I knew why. I thought perhaps that I had some sort of fight with Antonio. The battle appeared to have had raged all through the bathroom. The triple towel racks had been ripped form the wall and were on the floor, the towels were bloody. It was quite a scene. I felt if I showed Silva all this she might come back to Westfall with me and never speak of the summer of lust again. She had to. The evidence was here, the guy was a maniac. It was these soccer player types, they were an out of control bunch. I fixed my hair the best I could. Then I decided it was time to go find her and explain the truth about Antonio.

As I began to creep down the dark hallway I felt dizzy and had to lean against the wall. Then, I heard voices and saw a light coming from a partially open door. I realized I was on the second floor of the villa, right outside Silva's room.

I crept to the edge of the doorframe and listened. The door was open but I didn't want to reveal myself yet. Silva was whispering something to Antonio I was sure. I wondered if I had hurt him. I peeked. I couldn't see much. My eyes were a little blurred in the half-light from the alcohol and lack of spectacles.

"I can handle this," she said. "And stop touching me, I'm trying to help you."

I heard that one clearly. I slowly moved into the full light of the open door and then backed away suddenly when I smelled the cloves.

Silva was standing in between Oliver's long legs. She wore a robe, tied at the waist. Oliver's bad eye was all I could see of his face. He wore a patch but I couldn't tell the colors for the blood. The side of his face was a sheen of thin red. Silva was starting to clean the wound, her back to me.

"Oli, it's not that bad. He just cut your brow," she said.

"I can't believe he hit me."

"He didn't know it was you Oli. He was going after Antonio."

She had a cloth and a bottle of something in her hand. I watched as she dabbed the cloth and wiped his face. I leaned backward up against the wall to steady myself. I could not believe what I was hearing. I looked in again, and debated whether to go inside and apologize.

She lifted up his eye patch and a pool of blood that had formed inside it flowed out and down his face.

"Shit," Silva said and started cleaning him up all over again.

In a minute he was clean but she kept holding the cloth on the cut above his eye. I couldn't look away. My vision seemed to miraculously clear as I realized what was taking place in front of me and what I had managed to do to Oliver, again. This was how he looked on that day of the accident when I leaned over his unconscious body--a small bloody mass of eye.

Silva leaned over to pick a towel up off the bed.

"Don't move," she said.

She tied the towel around his head and eye like a turban.

"Now lay back," she said to him and helped him stretch out on the bed.

"It's not that bad, just a cut really," she said.

"I can't actually feel that much over the eye. The nerves where damaged in that area in the operation," Oliver said.

After she had him comfortable she climbed up on top and straddled him. Then she slowly leaned over and kissed him gently on the cheek. Oliver's hands were up on her back under her robe and then at her waist, sliding her robe away and revealing her slim body. She was in his arms now, naked. For a long moment they were motionless, and silent, as was I. It seemed I stood there forever. Something was not right. I could see it and feel it but could not believe it. Then, slowly, she began to gently move on top of him, the way as she had moved on top of me the night before.

Oliver didn't stop her.

I left.

Δ Δ Δ

A wise person once said that the definition of insanity is to repeat the same action over and over and expect a different result. Perhaps, it is not insane after all, but perfectly human. I for one had managed to stay sane for the three years since I left Westfall Academy and to expect almost nothing from another human being other than what they easily revealed they could do. I had learned such simple things as Oliver had always known, that love will betray you, and if not love, then you will somehow betray yourself to make sure to get the job done. This was just the way of the wounded was my conclusion, so for years I had opted not to play, not to try at all. How I had come to expect in a few short days that the world or I had somehow changed was beyond me. Perhaps the slide into insanity is like the slide into wishful thinking, wishful seeing, and every other manner of self concocted fantasy of the heart. Whatever the case, life was suddenly and ruthlessly once again clear to me. So it was easy to swiftly close myself up and cut her out and go. I even imagined I had risen above blame, anger and vengeance.

  I never told them about what I saw. So my last two days in Italy went smoothly. They claimed Oliver had been hurt by Antonio while he defended me after I lurched at Antonio on the dance floor. It had been the shortest fight in history since I had fallen on my knees and side and then on my head before I could even reach the bastard. I apologized to Oliver for the trouble. I realized that he and Silva had carried me upstairs to the bathroom after I had passed out on the dance floor. I had gotten sick in their arms, they said, and they had removed my shirt. They had taken care of me. I had put up a noble fight in the bathroom after I was sick they said. We all laughed about it.

  Silva tried to make me stay with her in Italy. But I unattached myself from her easily. She kissed me goodbye at the airport and tried her best smile on me. I smiled back, but I never budged, not even as her eyes lit up and she searched for a shred of soul inside of mine. She seemed confused by my sudden distance. It was so simple to do. One just stopped giving from the heart.

∆ ∆ ∆

When I returned home, it was the third week of September and my father was trying to sell the house in Westfall. I had been gone nine days and I expected my world in Westfall to have remained unchanged. But it never happens that way. At the very least, streets and stores feel different, and perhaps the worst is finding a "For Sale" sign outside your house.

My father hadn't actually lived in the house for years; he stayed in an apartment on Beacon Hill in Boston. I had rented a place. Our family custom and luxury had been for my father and I to meet at the house in Westfall for dinner and talk once every week. My father said it had to come to an end. That we needed to move on and let a young family move into the house. I told him I would live in the house and take care of the yard, everything, if he held onto it.

"I'll commute into school by train," I said.

"Then what?" he said. "What will we do, keep it forever?"

I saw his point, but told him the house needed fixing up before it could be sold. I wanted at least the school year and summer to do it. We were standing out on the back porch, looking over the river. It was our favorite place to be in the house and I had brought him out there on purpose.

"Besides, where else would we meet if not in this house?"

"We can't do this forever, Philip. A whole house just so we can talk is excessive."

That, in my opinion, depended on what one talked about.

I wondered if my mother had been there on the porch with us who she would have agreed with. My father, who wanted to let the final parts go, or myself, who held to last the shiny fragments like an old crow.

Δ  Δ  Δ

The summer after we all graduated from Westfall Academy I spent in Vermont alone with my Uncle Bernard. I remember I went back to what I knew. My life was once again filled with my familiar lonely routines. I ran five miles around the island every morning and read a novel at night. During the day I worked with Bernard on various projects and late every afternoon I went out to round up the horses. While I was walking them home I had plenty of time to think. It was only among those big animals that I ever spoke out loud about what really happened. I still don't know why, but out there on the path, while walking with Jerry, my favorite horse I could admit and say it to myself.

"I was the one who wounded Oliver Jerry. With a stupid piece of fruit. I knocked out half his world. And sometimes, I think I meant to do it."

Jerry didn't care much that I had done it, or if he did, he kept it to himself. It was comforting to be with him and the other horses. I had always been closer to them than most people it seemed.

Later that September I moved into my college dorm room and met Jake, my roommate. I got lucky, Jake was a good friend to me even though I largely ignored him at first. In those first few months of school my father was traveling a lot and sometimes I would take the train home from Cambridge. It was hard for me to stay in the house alone for too long though. But I did it sometimes anyway.

Once, I went to visit old teachers and younger friends at Westfall, but it felt like a sad thing to do, they with their own lives and hinting that I should be out creating a new one for myself. The problem was I didn't really know how to do that and never had.
Luckily one night in November Jake asked me again if I wanted to go play pool with him.

"Philip," he said. "This is the last time I am going to ask."

Jake had been diligently establishing a social circle for himself and he knew I needed to be a part of it. He was from Detroit, and old for a freshman, twenty, and had made some older friends right from the start.

"You only get a few chances Philip, to really make it happen. If you miss it, you're out. So why not come on out with us."

That was how my new life began. That night Jake introduced me to Andre, a senior studying Russian literature and the hairiest man I had ever seen. He wore a beard because the alternative was too much work, he said. Then there was Claudia, a junior studying art history who looked to be a woman out of an Italian renaissance painting: long blond hair pulled back and braided, smooth alabaster skin, lithe, but stable and graceful. There were several others I met too, but they faded. The core was the four of us, and within a month I was a permanent member. I must admit, I was proud of myself. I had forgotten Silva and Oliver both. I had moved on as one is likely to do when given no alternative.

Then, in late October, Oliver called me. I had not heard anything since they left after the graduation party. Not even a post card. I happened to be home in Westfall that day.

"I have to learn everything over again Philip. I can't even draw the same way!" he said.

Oliver didn't sound well. He was out of breath, like he had been climbing stairs before he called me.

"What's wrong Oli?"

"Everything. I can't do this Philip."

"Do what?"

"I can't paint, I can't draw, I can't see the way I used to and I miss your dreams Philip."

I took the phone away from my ear and took a deep breath. I had never heard Oliver sound this way. Even if I didn't exactly understand how he used to see things, this was still what I had always feared would happen. And yet, he needed me.

"You were working in Italy I assume?"

"I wasn't, Silva doesn't even know. I didn't want to worry her."

"I'm really sorry."

"You were right, Philip. I should have stayed with you. It would have been better."

I didn't know what to say.

"Philip?"

"Oli, you can stay with me now, if you need to," I said. "We can work this out together." He would have a room, set up a studio. Suddenly I saw it all.

"I thought it would come back, Philip. You know, on its own. The ability to recall everything perfectly like I use to."

He wasn't hearing me.

"Listen Oli, come up here. I'll get everything ready and we can beat this thing together. I know we can."

No, I was in school, he said, and he would just be in the way. He only needed to tell someone who would understand what he once had and why he couldn't work now. He was going to drop out of school. It was never right for him anyway. He said he needed to go back to the beginning, to learn to see all over again. I argued against it. I told him to wait a few days and think about it. I would come down to New York and visit. What would he do for money? What about Silva? All these things, I said, and still, I lost him.

Oliver disappeared onto the streets of New York. He didn't communicate with me, or anyone, for months. But on New Year's Eve a post-card arrived. He wrote saying he was fine, being taken care of. Soon after that, the cards began to trickle in, twice a month or so. It soon became clear to me that Oliver was travelling. He had become a vagabond, sketchbook in hand, and with each new postcard came some bizarre coincidence in his journey. He talked and made friends with everyone: bums, cops, senators, movie stars, beast tamers, boar hunters, circus people, people with golf clubs on their way to Florida, kids on their way back to school leaving Miami Beach looking haggard and spent, truck drivers, Europeans who always took him in as a fellow foreigner lost and dazed in America, a farmer from Nebraska, waitress from Alaska, a convenience store robber on the run looking for a hostage, and yet another thief who gave him some cash he had just scored, ten minutes earlier, from a hog dog salesman and who needed to share his victory and guilt. It went on and on and Oliver took it all in. He was on an adventure of Greek proportions it seemed. And every once in a while he wrote of a secret he had discovered about himself, a thing he had forgotten long ago that when he remembered the truth he had laughed for days. He never said what it was he remembered, only that it had changed how he saw the world forever and that he was grateful for the accident for that was what had helped him remember the truth. Sometimes I wondered if he had lost his mind. Finally, I just decided all this travel and talk of remembered secrets just helped him forget he could no longer hold the world still in his mind and record it exactly as he wanted.

For the next three years I received sporadic postcards from places all over the country and eventually the world. Over time they covered my walls and Jake, Andre and Claudia came to wonder about Oliver, who he was, and what his travels were all about. Sometimes over a game at the pool hall, Oliver would come up, like an old friend can, or perhaps a new card had arrived that day, and I would begin to tell of his most recent adventures. It was innocent enough at first, the telling of these stories, but eventually Oliver became a common subject during our games. We would be shooting eight ball and suddenly someone would invoke Oliver for luck.

"This one's for Oliver," Claudia would say, or , "Oliver willing I will sink this," from Andre. And then Jake would always be the one to ask for a story from me.

"Tell us about Oliver, Philip. What is he up to now."

I told more stories than I should have. Stories of his eccentric behavior, his passion for art and lust for life, and only slowly did I diverge from the truth. I admit, it was almost too easy for me. Oliver became mythical in proportion, stronger, faster, and more brilliant than perhaps he ever was in life. Yet, he suffered more as well. He became, like Odysseus, consumed with an undying passion to return home, to the time before the loss of his greatest love, his perfect vision of the world.

∆ ∆ ∆

It came in the mail. Silva wrote me a letter in early October to say they had lined up a show of Oliver's paintings in March in New York. Oliver had been showing his work in London and Milan for over a year. I hadn't known how well he had been doing in the art world in Europe. Well enough apparently for an Italian gallery director to arrange it all. Silva made it seem that Oliver was fast becoming the new young hit in the painting world. I didn't doubt it, Oliver always had it in him. But I waited to see what happened. These things have a way of falling through. I wrote a short letter back with my warmest regards. I expected they would visit at some point, but I didn't want her to think she could stay forever. I decided if they came to visit at all, it would be on my terms.

Not long after I sent off my letter Oliver sent me a postcard from Vienna. It looked much like the cards he used to write me when he first disappeared. He didn't mention his upcoming trip or recent successes in the galleries. I wondered if it was even true or if Silva had exaggerated the situation. It seemed Oliver preferred to be invisible, to vanish inside the work in the same way he covered over his subjects. I found it hard to believe he would allow fame to creep up on him.

I took my fall semester classes and worked on the house some. I decided to go ahead and clear out the basement for my father. He was living in the city and came out on weekends after work to help me take care of the yard or start up some new project. We had a deal, and I was indeed holding up my end of it. I had begun sanding down the wood floors which he and my mother hand danced over for years and left their mark.

"It has to be done," I said to my father. I knew he hadn't thought about the floors--of erasing the subtle evidence of his marriage and the love of his life.

"You're right, it has to be done," my father said, looking at the sanded floor in a sort of daze.

"And we need to take that old refrigerator in the cellar to the dump," I added.

"Right," he said.

"I'll have to call Andre in," I said.

But my father was hesitant about the help. Not because he didn't like owing people favors, he just thought our stuff should stay our stuff. But I convinced him the whale of a fridge was going nowhere without Andre's strength to get it up the stairs.

Δ  Δ  Δ

In was late November, Claudia, Andre, and myself, were down in the basement moving the fridge.

"This would be perfect," was the first thing Andre said after he descended the stairs.

"What?" I said.

"For a pool room...small windows, large empty space, and access to a fridge."

I'm not sure why I gave in so easily to the idea. After I returned from Italy I had refused to see anyone for two weeks. I said I was recovering from an illness, and in a way I was. When Andre and Claudia had come to check on me I remained quiet on the subject of my trip to Italy. They respected my need for silence.

After my first few weeks of isolation I went out to Jillian's pool hall and in general picked up where I had left off. Andre finally moved into Jake's new apartment instead of me since I had decided to live at the house. Eventually I told some simple lies about Italy, but never the truth. The Oliver stories were over, too, and everyone noticed the change. Claudia in particular could tell something had gone wrong while I was away. She was generous with her attention after my return, and I accepted her small touches on the arm, the warm smiles, and pointers in my pool game. She knew, as she always had, the condition of my heart. But despite this knowledge, she never tried to make me deliver up the truth.

It soon became inevitable that the basement would be converted into a pool hall. I needed a reason for my friends to visit me in Westfall, and they were more than willing to contribute. It took a long time to complete, a few months of weekends and most of the holiday season, with Andre helping me take loads of old junk to the dump. I was slow about sifting through the old books and papers. Andre was patient with me.

In January, while we were sifting through an old train trunk left over from my Great Grandfather's touring days I found a world atlas. I opened it and it randomly fell to the page revealing the peninsula that is Italy.

"Great," I said.

Andre looked over at it. "So...as I understand it, Philip, there was some kind of difficulty over in Europe."

"Sort of."

"Was anyone injured?"

"Nothing permanent, no."

I looked away from the map and down at my feet. It was so cold in the basement then that I could see my breath.

"You want more coffee?" I asked.

There was a long pause. Then he stood up. "Sure," he said, "I'll get it."

He went up the stairs and left me there to think it out on my own.

I don't know why I never told him about Italy. It wasn't our way. It was as if we, my college friends, had all silently agreed not to talk about those things that can't be expressed well. Claudia, perhaps, was somehow at the heart of our understanding. There was something about her, and how she played pool, which required a person to stay focused on the game despite appearing relaxed.

"All that can be said comes out on the felt," she once said to me about life. It was a fairly general and oversimplified statement, but I liked it none-the-less. Sometimes, I even chose to believe it.

It took us another three weekends before we were finally ready to paint the new basement pool hall, but we did it all in one day once we committed to the colors. Andre was anxious to finish because he had had his eye on an antique table in the city. Claudia had gone and done her job by playing a few games then gave the table her blessing.

"Buy it, Andre, before it's gone," she said, "It's perfect."

He did, actually we went in on it together, and had it delivered and set up.

My father reluctantly gave his okay. I argued it would add value to the house. "A house must be furnished," I said. "That is, if it is expected to sell itself."

In late February Jake came in to help with the heating. He installed a permanent electric wall unit, and by then we had made up the room well, painted the concrete floors and stained the wood ceilings and hung pool hall lights over the table. It was simple, elegant, no frills. Jake managed to fix the refrigerator, so it stayed to hold beer for Jake and Andre, and water for Claudia, who never drank when she played. I bought an old coffee machine from a couple having a yard sale down the street and brought it down. We were set. The poolroom was complete; and it was on that afternoon, when we had all decided to christen the table, that Oliver suddenly appeared, ragged, spent, and delirious at my door.

∆ ∆ ∆

I was in the basement with Jake and Andre. We were all watching Claudia run the table when it happened. The phone rang and I hustled up to the kitchen to get it. It was Silva. I had not spoken to her in seven months. She was upset and sounded desperate. She tried to hide it but I could hear it under her voice.

"Hello, Philip, how are you?"

These were nice words to begin with. They were also the only ones she faked.

"Silva, what's wrong?"

"I woke up this morning, Philip, and he was gone! Do you have him?"

"Who?"

"Philip!" She was almost yelling at me.

She was terrified Oliver had vanished for good. She said he was very nervous about the show in New York and didn't want any part of it. There had been a disagreement the night before.

"Philip, what am I supposed to do? The show opens in five days and if he isn't back it will be a total failure. They will think I'm a fool."

I assumed "they" was the gallery and tried to calm her down by saying they were used to dealing with artists. Then I felt Claudia's hand on my arm. I turned and smiled at her. She wrote a short note on the pad by the phone.

*Oliver.* It said.

I mouthed back. *No, Silva.*

She shook her head no and wrote again as I continued to talk with Silva. I promised her Oliver would be there. I said things to calm her that I couldn't be sure about myself. By then she was yelling at me about Oliver like I was somehow responsible. I had never heard her this way. I figured she must have laid out all the money they saved in Italy for this trip. Her plan, I gathered from her fragmented story, was that the show would go so well that they would finally be set to live on their own. It was a plan, and it was falling apart and that meant she would once again have to depend on someone.

I looked at Claudia's note.

*I think Oliver is on the back porch.*

I pulled the phone away from my face and covered it with my hand.

"Really?"

"Yes."

He was there. I saw him through the kitchen sliding glass door standing on the porch. I panicked and handed the phone to Claudia.

"Here. Introduce yourself. Get her to calm down, will you, but don't tell her he's here."

Claudia gave short nod and I heard her cool voice suddenly break into Silva's tirade. I went to the sliding glass door. The sun had set behind Heron Hill across the river and the sky was lit with long fingers of color. I struggled for a moment thinking of what to do. His back was to me. To ignore him would mean he would wait on the back porch until I came out to get him. I wanted to get everyone out of the house before he came in. I was not ready for my two worlds to meet. But then Oliver turned and was at the door. I just stood there and looked at him, then I opened the door and he fell in. I helped him walk to the couch in the living room where he rested for a moment. I could feel how hot his body was. I heard Claudia's explanation that "Philip was cooking" and had to attend to dinner before it burned. Then she was calling me, saying Silva wanted to speak to me again. I left Oliver on the couch for the moment and went back to finish the conversation.

"Philip," she said, when I was back on, "who was that and what is going on?"

"Just a friend, we had a sudden grease fire situation, but no big deal. I got it under control."

"What's her name?"

"Claudia."

"Well, I didn't appreciate you handing me off."

"Listen Silva. I have to go. I have guests. I am sorry about Oliver, but I am sure it will all work out. And I swear if he shows up here I'll call you immediately. Now what is your number?"

There was a moment of silence, as it seemed she registered the resolve in my voice. Then she gave me the number and tried to ask how my life was. I said I would call and tell her later. She said my invitation to the show was in the mail. I said good-bye.

When I looked for Oliver he and Claudia were gone. He was in my room. She had covered him up in my bed and found a thermometer to put in his mouth.

"Okay," I said, sitting down on the other side of the bed from her, with Oliver between us. "How is he?"

Claudia, as if woken from a dream looked up at me. "Sick," she said. "What did you tell Silva?"

"I explained who you were and that I would call if he showed up." Claudia raised her eyebrows.

"Well, you heard her. She was a lunatic."

"True, maybe it's best she doesn't know, at least until he gets a little better."

"Exactly."

Oliver mumbled something unintelligible.

We both looked at him. His one eye was open. I had thought he had fallen asleep or passed out.

"Oli, what is wrong with you?"

"Nothing. I'm just tired. Long walk from New York."

I saw Claudia smile at this.

She took the thermometer from his mouth. "103. No wonder."

"It's a little heat is all," he said.

"Yes, I can see that," she said. "Philip get a cold cloth."

"Don't tell her I'm here Philip, please."

I turned and looked at him. He was pleading, and looked, in his own way, as desperate as Silva had sounded. I wasn't going to be easy on him either.

"I can't lie for you forever, Oli. I'll tell her in the morning."

Claudia gave me a look of disapproval, as if to say my words had been too harsh. Maybe they had. Oliver closed his eye on me.

I went down to the basement to retrieve Andre and Jake.

"It's Oliver. He's here and he's ill."

They came up to see Oliver, and for a moment, all four of us stood around the bed and watched him sleeping. For them, he must have seemed like a character risen to life out of a book. To my friends, I knew Oliver had always been a fabrication. Before they left, Oliver woke, opened his one good eye and surveyed the room. He saw us all standing over him like carrion birds, and Claudia sitting there beside him. He reached out his right hand for Claudia's. I had never seen Claudia this way. She was moved by him. I saw it in her eyes and her face, which so seldom went soft. She rubbed Oliver's hand like she had known him for years and had sat by him like this through all his troubles. Perhaps she had in her own way. What, after all, was the truth about Oliver anymore? I had given up trying to understand him after Italy. Perhaps my own version, the one I gave to them, was more authentic than any factual story could ever have been.

Later, down in the kitchen, they were preparing to leave. It was almost midnight by this time and Silva had called back twice to check if Oliver had arrived. I let the answering machine deal with her and found myself enjoying a strange sort of pleasure while listening to her. I stood over the answering machine and didn't even feel the desire to pick up the phone as she rambled on about her troubles.

"Please pick up," she would say. "I can feel you listening to me Philip. Don't think I don't know what you are doing."

Andre was out in his jeep waiting for Claudia. Jake had left an hour earlier because he had to work in the morning. We were standing at the front door, Claudia and myself. She asked if she should stay. I told her I could handle it.

"He will be fine," I said.

"You're sure," she said.

"Even if he is half as strong as my stories made him out to be then he will be fine."

"But Philip..."

"What?"

Claudia looked at me as if trying to sum something up.

"Nothing. You're right. He will be fine. I'm sure. Just...keep an eye on him."

"I will, I will," I said and ushered her out the door. I thought it was sweet how much Claudia had taken to him. She had always liked the Oliver I invented for her, always wanted to meet him more than the rest.

It felt good to have the house back again. It felt good to have Oliver upstairs in his condition and Silva far away in New York in hers. I had always suspected that a day like this would come. For once, things were under my control.

I went into the living room and sat in a lazy chair, where I figured on sleeping. I hoped that my two Olivers could somehow become one in a way that set me free from both of them.

Δ   Δ   Δ

The next morning Oliver came down looking better, but not perfect. I had made coffee and filled the house with the familiar promise of a good day to come. I was out on the porch reading my way through the local paper. There is always an odd assortment of petty crimes, successes, and other wonderful true life stories. The river was flowing by, which was reassuring.

It was Sunday and the sun was out making it just warm enough to sit and enjoy myself. I think I remember church bells ringing as Oliver came out onto the porch.

"It's like spring out here," he said to me after taking a deep breath through his nose.

I asked him how he was feeling and he looked me over.

"Was I not feeling well when I arrived?" he said.

I nodded.

"I don't remember a bit of it."

I told him that was not a good sign, but he was convinced that an illness not remembered is an illness not suffered.

"That's ridiculous Oliver."

"You taught me that Philip," he said and then headed down the porch stairs. "The river," he said. "I must have a swim."

"What? Oliver it's freezing."

He began taking off his clothing. I never could stop him from doing anything he really wanted to do. On his way across the lawn he leaned over and dipped his hand into the fire-pit and scooped up some ashes. He held them up and then turned around to show me, ash sifted through his fingers and drifting to the ground below.

"It's good to be back Philip," he said to me.

I nodded and lifted my coffee cup.

In the river he took up some water, and proceeded to smooth the ashes all over his now naked self. This was not that unusual. I had seen this sort of thing on television. I think it is done in India, and what's more I had seen Oliver covered in paint half a dozen times, this was just a variation on a theme. Yet, I decided he might not be all-better after his forgotten illness. I kept an eye on him as he waded out into the water and turned to face the current.

The Westfall River never moves fast. Oliver stood up to his waist and let his arms hang back in the water. Slowly he inched farther out into the middle of the river. You might imagine that a man who had lived as a vagabond all over the world could take care of himself in a river. In his years of traveling about I am sure he had a number of opportunities in which to brush with death. Why he had to choose my house, my river, on my Sunday morning to exercise his right to blow death a kiss, I don't know. I advise that you *never* lift the newspaper over your line of sight when your half-crazed best friend is wading in deep water. It is what they are all waiting for. A chance to slip away.

The fastest part of any river is underneath the surface. There is a cylindrical tunnel-like current in the middle that runs quicker than any of the water surrounding it. If the water moves on top, even just a little, then it's a little faster right below, just about where you were thinking it might become calm and safe it is moving along.

Oliver didn't make the appropriate, I-am-going-under-now noise: the quick deep inhalation of breath. I don't know what he was thinking. All I saw was the last tuft of blond hair slip under and I immediately spilled my coffee all over the paper and my lap. I launched myself off the porch.

I was wearing my robe, slippers, and shorts underneath. All but my shorts came off by the time I reached the river. I stopped at the bank and looked for signs of him swimming. I had to adjust where I jumped in. I figured he had let himself float down towards Christopher Bridge because there were no ripple marks from feet kicking. This floating thing was an old pastime of ours, something we did senior spring once or twice back at Westfall before I injured him.

I headed under into the coldest water I had ever been in and down into the center of the river. I went into the faster current hoping to overtake him. Down there something happened to me. I believe now that it was the cold getting deep into me in a way it had not in many years. The cold took me places I had no intention of going. It was as if a memory swept over me, but so powerfully as to be a dream.

Δ  Δ  Δ

*It is snowing. I am watching the flakes sift down through the light of the flood lamp perched like a gargoyle outside my window. The room surrounds me like a flannel blanket and snow comes and goes against the window in slow languid waves. The dogs are asleep on the floor at the foot of my bed. I am eleven years old. I am waiting for my parents to come home from a New Year's Eve party. I am still there, waiting.*

Δ  Δ  Δ

I had to come up from the water. When I did the dream was gone and I had no time to think about it, nor did I want to. Oliver was nowhere to be seen.

I dove back beneath and what I touched first were his hands, held out to me. He was floating along stretched out like a flying super-hero, only backwards, with the current pulling him gently towards Christopher Bridge. As soon as I touched his hands he grabbed on to me and we sailed along connected at the wrists, secure and steady as trapeze artists. I had to go for air so we came up together. I did not save his life, not this time, or any other time. On the surface he was all smiles and his one shrunken eye-lid was cold and wrinkled up like an old woman's face.

"Shall we float down to the bridge?" he said.

"No! God, Oliver, I'm not going anywhere near that bridge!"

So he let go, submerged himself, and swam away from me like a frog. I reached out instinctively in the dark water and suddenly found him solid and resisting the current. He had hold of something, a root perhaps, and I had hold of him. At some point, about when my lungs were ready to give out I let go and it happened again, I was in a dream as I began to surface.

Δ   Δ   Δ

*I am floating out of my body, floating above Christopher Bridge and it is that night, New Year's Eve night. I see them in my father's blue corvette. They are on their way home from the New Year's Eve party. It is the New Year. Now they are crossing Christopher. I am floating above them, I am helpless, like a feather kept in the air by the wind, but desperately trying to descend. It is too late. I see it happen, the oncoming truck swerves out of control on the ice. They are the last car on the bridge in a line of three, their friends ahead of them are safe, they are home soon, now, beyond this moment which is frozen forever. There is no mistake, no error anywhere, everything occurs perfectly, exactly as it had to, as it should have, must have, or it would not have.*

*The old corvette spreads out in waves, the doors, like two wings suddenly opening, are ripped off the body of the car, glass is shot out along the icy road like silver coins that pop up and out into the night and then fall to the water below. It is instantaneous. She is crushed under a storm of blue fragments. She is spilling out into the night in a great pour--she is my mother rolling away along the surface of a cold black river.*

Δ  Δ  Δ

Then it's over. When I break the surface, I am alone. Oliver has drifted. I am gasping for air, searching for the shore. I swim for my life. I can barely breath.

What I found was a rock some thirty yards up from Christopher Bridge. Oliver appeared beside me soon after I was secure.

"Are you alright Philip?"
"I'm not going any further Oliver. This is it for me."
"Can you make it to the shore?"
"I think so."
"I will make sure."

I swam to the shore and Oliver swam beside me. I crawled out but he stayed behind.

Oliver never wished to leave the water once he was in it. He always wanted to float, surrounded in darkness, like a sea turtle, he would say. He loved darkness, no friction, and the smooth of water, like the polished side of a shark's tooth, he once said.

"I will swim the rest of the way for you Philip," he said.

"No you will not," I told him firmly.

I tried to reach him but he was gone.

I watched him go, then I could no longer see him. He had vanished beneath. Perhaps beneath the bridge itself. I sat and looked at the river. I was shivering. I was sure I would never see him or anyone I loved again.

When I returned from Italy I felt the same way. I spent some time down in the basement in those first few days, sitting near the boiler and smelling the autumn air mixing the heat and cold into a strange set of temperatures. I was riffling through the files like never before, thinking I might be able to find some explanation in the minutia of old letters and report cards of how I ever became so completely blind to the dangers of love.

Then I found it. I had never seen it, or been shown it before. I don't even know how my father got it or why. It was a horrible thing. Perhaps he insisted. He had friends who were doctors. It was a report of some kind, a medical report I think. The kind relatives are never meant to see. But it did not say *dead on arrival* as I expected and had been told. There was a whole list of events, medical terms, things I believe they tried to do to save my mother's life. It said: wounds to the chest, glass, rupture, puncture, and finally, collapse. These were the words used to describe the state she existed in for twelve minutes after they brought her into the emergency room. Then, indeed, alone, with strangers pouring over her open body, she had finally died, instantly, as they had told me.

∆ ∆ ∆

Before lunch my father called. I supplied him with all the relevant details and convinced him the situation with Oliver was under control. Then I made my call to Silva. I told her the news. That Oliver had arrived in the early morning cold and sick. As expected, she was furious that I hadn't called her immediately. She said she had been worried all morning and wondered why I hadn't answered her other calls from the night before. I told her I had gone out to get some medicine for Oliver, and had done some food shopping, since the house had not been lived in much. I wondered if this was how she felt in Italy, this easy sort of lying that just dances off the tongue.

"Okay," I said. "Yes, come up as soon as you can."

She had already checked for flights and said the only shuttle with seats was after the rush hour and so she wouldn't be able to leave until nine that night.

"I'll be there to pick you up. I promise."

She sounded a little less desperate after she had her plans set and knew Oliver was in custody, as she called it. I promised I would not let him go. I hung up and felt good. I had the rest of the afternoon to think about the night to come. I knew I didn't want her coming back to the house and I wasn't sure how I wanted my two worlds to meet. I needed a plan and decided to call Claudia and confide in her.

"I don't know Claudia, honest. I didn't know what was going on when I left Italy and I still don't. Silva has an agenda."

I was pacing the kitchen in circles and stopping at the sliding door every so often to look out at the river for Oliver.

"I think she just wants Oliver with her no matter the cost to anybody else."

"And she needs the money?"

"I think it goes way beyond that now. She simply needs him to live."

"But what about Oliver?"

"I don't know. Oliver is Oliver, Claudia. He is the kind of person who just floats down a river naked."

"That is not an answer, Philip."

"It's all I have." Then I told her I needed some help handling Silva and I would get back to her once I had figured my plan out. Claudia said she would help.

After Oliver returned he spent the rest of the afternoon asleep on the couch in the living room. I kept checking on him. I was worried. He had arrived wearing the bare minimum, no vest, no sport coat, just his loafers, a pair of cut off old army pants and a white T-shirt rolled up to the shoulders. I hadn't noticed it until he stripped, but he had lost weight. He was not well, that was clear.

Silva called around five again to check on him. I didn't answer the phone. She left me her flight information on the machine and sounded nervous. Please keep him there, she said. Then she added that she would like to have a quiet night alone at the house, just the three of us. She said there were things we should all talk about. Like the future, she said. She had something important to tell me about Oliver. And she needed my help—okay Philip, she said. Can we do that?

∆ ∆ ∆

      I left Oliver sleeping and went for a walk at sunset. I went along the river towards school. I scanned the river and saw images from the unintended morning swim. I thought about the past and tried to shed light on the unfathomable feelings I had for Oliver. While I stood there watching the river something tried to change inside me, give itself up, and make room for the both of them at once, the way it was and not the way I wanted it. But I couldn't.
I walked down to Christopher Bridge where my father had often walked with my mother years ago. I stood for a bit, looking about at this place where he had both found and lost his true love.
      The sun was setting and a new cold drew itself down on the world. Winter was slow leaving that year. The news said a cold front was heading in. There was even a possibility of some snow by dawn, a few inches perhaps. Then, for some reason, as I stood on the bridge, I remembered the story Oliver had told me when I arrived in Italy. The one about him almost making love under the statue of Venus to some mystery woman. It was about he and Silva of course. I knew that now. What I didn't understand was why he told me at all or why he had refused her. Perhaps it was his way of trying to warn me about her, about love, and maybe even about himself, too. Whatever he meant to show me, it was beyond my understanding, Oliver spoke in actions, I in words. We were languages apart.

∆ ∆ ∆

That evening, while Silva was in transit from JFK to Logan, I was in the house, pacing. When I was out on my walk Oliver had slipped away. I was nervous that maybe he had finally gone into the river and left for good. I was still waiting for him when I saw Andre's jeep pull in, and riding shotgun was Oliver. He stayed in the jeep while Andre came in.

"So what happened?"

"I found him walking away. He was about a mile off."

"Good, that's good, so he didn't try to run when he saw you?"

"No."

"Good."

"What is wrong with him Philip?"

"I don't know. He seems restless. But he won't talk about it. He won't even admit that he's ill."

Andre nodded.

Then I reviewed my plan for the night with him. We were to pick up Claudia at her place first and then Andre would drop us off on Landsdown Street. Jake would meet us there and Andre would pick up Silva with Oliver and bring them all back to the Jillian's. From there, things could proceed at my pace, and not Silva's.

Δ Δ Δ

When Andre and Silva arrived at Jillian's pool hall I could see Andre had been working on her. It was perfect. She was beautiful, and he enjoyed his assignment. Andre ordered rum and cokes for them both after our initial hello.

I could see as I left for an open pool table with Jake that Silva was trying to get my attention and talk to me. I pretended not to see her and she was too courteous to just excuse herself from Andre's charm and follow me.

The pool hall was mostly full and the bar busy. It was how I wanted it, plenty of people around. I was a little nervous about Andre telling my old Oliver stories to Silva, but then I realized she wouldn't know if they were true or not. I, not her, after all, was the one who had received all the cards from Oliver during his travels.

Jake broke. If he had a truly excellent break, he could sometimes run the table. He listened quietly as we played our game and I told him the situation.

"But what is the goal here, Philip?"

"I suppose to just exasperate her."

"I see."

I ignored him for the moment. I was looking over at Oliver and Claudia. They had found a set of chairs in a corner and were talking. They looked serious.

"Philip?"

"What?" I said.

"Your turn."

"Hmmm," Jake said as I missed an easy shot. He lined up the six ball and sunk it in with a delicate touch. He was kind enough to drop the subject of Silva.

Silva and Andre came over to watch our game.

"Hi," Silva said.

"Did you sleep on the plane?" I asked.

She smiled, and bumped her shoulder into mine, and ignored my question. She smelled sweet as always.

"Philip?" she said.

It was my shot.

"Hold on," I said and walked away from her.

I cleaned up the table and Andre was going to challenge me, but then he decided to fetch drinks for all of us. "Silva, lets get some drinks for these two." He took her arm and off she went looking back over her shoulder at me. I smiled and had that same feeling of pleasure I had when she was talking into my answering machine and I didn't pick up.

I looked over towards Oliver and Claudia and saw that Claudia was holding Oliver's hand now. Then, as if they knew I was looking she leaned over and touched her forehead with his. It was the strangest and most effortless display of communication I had ever seen. It was something I could never have done. I looked over at Silva. She was looking too, and then at me. I shrugged my shoulders at her, turned my back. I concentrated on the new game. I played fabulously. I felt good and it showed.

"I hate to spoil your fun but we have a development?" Jake said.

"What?"

"She's leaving."

I turned around. Silva was heading for the ladies room. Andre gave me a nod from the bar. I nodded back. I had things just about how I wanted them. Both Oliver and Silva were away from me and each other. Claudia came over to challenge me to a game and Jake took Oliver downstairs to the dueling piano bar for a spell. Oliver said he had never seen pianos duel and was excited about it.

"Go ahead," I said when they all looked at me as if to ask for permission. "We will come down after this game."

"So, what do you think of them?" I asked Claudia.

"Oliver is nice, but dying."

"Oh?"

"Yes."

"Don't listen to him Claudia. He is always being reborn, too, it's this idea he has about artists--always evolving up the spiral, he says."

"He rants on about, Silva too. She has these plans for the summer."

She missed one and I was up.

"Really?"

"She hasn't told you yet?"

I held back from taking my next shot after sinking the seven ball.

"I don't happen to know everything about them."

"Philip, don't get so touchy. I just figured she might have told you."

"Well she didn't, not yet anyway. I've been avoiding her."

I could tell by her smile that Claudia was amused with me. It made me settle down a little. Claudia knew how to bait me, and always got me heated when she wanted to prove a point.

"Her plan is for all three of you to drive across the country: Chicago, Taos, and then San Francisco."

"For God's sake, why?"

"To set up a network of galleries for his work."

"Damn, she's planning the next step even before the show opens?"

"I imagine she is thinking about her future, Philip."

Claudia had taken over and cleared the table while we talked. Every now and then she missed on purpose so I could do something besides drink and stand there.

On my next turn at the table I sunk five and felt good about it. It took my mind off the plan to cross the country. I figured things must be bad between the two of them if Silva actually wanted me along.

"I bet Oliver doesn't even like the plan," I said.

But Claudia was concentrating on a difficult shot. I looked up and around. Andre was no longer at the bar and I couldn't see Silva anywhere in the hall either.

"Did you see where Silva went?" I asked Claudia after she finished.

"Back to the bar."

"I don't see them over there."

Claudia cleared the table quickly. Then I took the balls back, paid for our time and then we went to the bar. There was a crowd there but they weren't in it. Claudia thought Silva and Andre must have gone down to the piano bar to find Oliver. I wasn't so sure, so I waited behind while she went down to look for them. I watched the pool hall. Then I walked out onto the curb and waited a few minutes. Nothing, and no one in the piano bar either.

Not far down the street was the club we often went to after we played pool. Andre knew all the doormen so we got in free. I walked down and stood talking to Eric. He said he had seen Claudia go in, but not Andre.

Inside at a table in a corner I saw Claudia and Jake and made my way over.

"What's going on?" I said.

"Oliver skipped out while I was down at the piano bar," Jake said.

"What?"

"Silva flipped out when she came down and found him gone," Claudia added.

I pulled myself in closer to hear Jake's rendition of what happened. He said Oliver and he had gone down together but that Oliver wanted to have a smoke outside and said to go ahead in and get a table.

"So I did and when I came out to look for him the doorman said he had gone off with a squatter who was hanging around across the street by the parking lot."

"A squatter?"

"Yeah," Claudia said. "You know, people without homes, who wander around."

"Yeah I know. I just..."

"Silva went ballistic," Claudia said. "She and Andre are out looking for them right now.

After a few minutes of silence Claudia said she was heading home, that she didn't think Oliver was coming back, not from what he said to her earlier.

"Why? What did he say?" I asked.

"I think you should go home, Philip."

"What, why?"

"Look, Andre has got Silva. Do you really want to be here when she gets back and is empty handed? Who do you think she's going to blame?"

She had a point. Jake seemed to be in agreement.

"I'll stay and wait for them," he said. "I have the least to do with any of this."

"Plus, if Oliver is going to come back it's likely he will show up in Westfall again," Claudia said.

"Did he say that?"

"No. He didn't say. He just said he had had enough of all this and that he was leaving."

"That's it?"

"Yes," she said, annoyed at my pestering.

It hadn't ended how I expected, but it was good enough. Maybe Silva would even stay with Andre for the night. It would make it all easier, which I decided was how I preferred it.

Δ Δ Δ

It wasn't until Claudia and I had left, and I was on my way home to Westfall that I began to feel something stirring. We were sharing a taxi. Jake had left my car at his apartment and I didn't want to bother getting it. For some reason I was not satisfied with the results of the night.

"Not to worry," Claudia said reading my mood and kissing me on the cheek when we got to Harvard Square where she lived.

"Jake and Andre can take care of themselves and if they find him they will let us know."

"Right," I said and smiled.

"Philip. You did well tonight. I think you showed them both that you have a life."

"You think so?"

"Yes," she said and turned to me and looked into my eyes. But for some reason I didn't feel the same confidence she had in me. I just didn't want her to get out of the cab.

And then I did something I had never done before.

"Claudia," I said. "Can I come up?"

She looked at me long and hard as if she were trying to work out what I meant. I expected she might laugh at me, but she didn't. Instead she put her hand on my arm. Then she leaned over and kissed me softly on the lips.

"It's no wonder they love you so, Philip," she said. "But I think you should go home. This night isn't over for you yet." She reached up and pushed the hair from my forehead and turned to leave the cab.

"What do you mean?"

"Just be flexible, Philip," she said looking down at me smiling before she closed the door.

"Goodnight," I said, "I'll try."

I lied of course. I didn't try to be more flexible. I reveled in the new rigidity that was slowly descending over me like a heavy snowfall. What was she talking about anyway? Claudia didn't understand the whole story. All the way home I was courting my vindictive self. I would win this game, once and for all.

∆ ∆ ∆

At home I made myself a stiff rum and coke, drank it, and then promptly fell asleep in an easy chair by the fireplace. When I awoke it was to Silva sitting on the arm of the chair, her hands, one in my hair and one rubbing my chest. She was here to fetch me, she said. Then she was in my lap and laying herself over me like liquid. She kissed me, and for a moment I forgot. Then I remembered Italy and stood up abruptly.

"I'm sorry Philip. I knocked on the door but you were asleep, so I came in."

I ignored her. She was going to try and tell me how it was. I could feel it coming.

"Did you find Oliver?"

She didn't answer but just looked around at the house.

"No. But I will. I can feel he is close by." She said and tossed her hair back.

"Do you want a drink or something?" I said.

"Sure."

She was already drunk, but not enough for me to forgive her anything.

"What have you been doing?" I asked.

"Driving around with the guys."

I made her a gin and tonic and opened a soda for myself. She slipped off her shoes, sat on the couch and pulled her legs up.

She stared at me and smiled. Then she looked down at her lap and her hair fell over her face as she said it.

"Philip, I really do love you." She looked up at me. Then rose to her feet and began walking toward me. I backed into the mantle.

"You have to believe me." She took another step forward and came so close I could smell the sweet alchemy of perfume and alcohol again. Then, she leaned her forehead against my chest, her arms still down at her sides.

"Philip, please," she said. "I can't lose both of you, not again. It has always been this way Philip."

We stood together for some time after I wrapped my arms around her. I didn't know what else to do. For a moment, I almost believed it could be true. Then she began again: The negotiations. She let go of me and stepped back.

"Oliver's not a threat to you and I, Philip. Only to himself."

"I know," I said.

"He wants to disappear again. Go back to being a vagabond."

She paused to look down at a run in her black stockings. I knew Oliver wanted to escape her and I didn't care why. The conversation always went back to him. I didn't understand how she could continue to pretend they weren't lovers, and that it didn't matter. How she could keep lying to me.

"Philip?" she said suddenly. "Tell me what have I done to make him run from me? Did he tell you anything?"

"No, nothing."

She rubbed her eyes with her fingers and I noticed how little makeup she wore. How beautiful she seemed when she tried least to be that way. The window closest to the couch was open a bit and the night was cold. I walked over and closed it.

"I'm tired," she said. "Maybe I could sleep here?"

"Silva? Andre is outside," I said. I could see his jeep out there like a buffalo wintering in the drive.

"Oh my God, they are waiting for me out there? How long have I been in here? We have to go. Come, Philip, please? Come with me, help me find Oliver and convince him to stay with us. You and me, like it was at Westfall, and in Italy. We could live here, all three of us, together."

"I don't think so Silva."

"Yes please, come with me, Philip."

"No, it's just not for me."

She was in front of me again.

"I told them I would be right back," she said and reached up to kiss me. I took a step back. She stared at me for a long time. Then she walked from the living room into the kitchen and I heard her glass find its place on the counter. I heard her go through the den and into the dancing room.

"House looks nice Philip," she called. "Empty."

I walked into the dancing room. There was no furniture except a coat rack in the corner near the front door and a lamp. She ran her hand over the marble edge of the mantle.

I turned on the corner lamp. The light spread low and dim across the room. Silva walked into the middle of the room, and looked down at the wood. She knelt. The scratches and scuffmarks from years of dancing were mostly gone. She stared at what remained.

"Why are you trying to sand it away Philip?" she said running her hand over the floor.

"I made a deal with my father. He wants to sell the house."

She had placed her shoes down next to her. Her one hand slowly moved over the dusty surface of the wood.

"Do you know Oli will leave me if I can't keep you?" she said.

It wasn't a question really. I knew it and so did she. I was standing beside her looking down at the hard floor.

"If it comes to that, yes."

She stood up slow and unbalanced. I helped her. She turned and faced me with no space between us this time. Her chest was lightly pressed against mine.

"Come with us?" she said. "We could all be together. I promise it will be okay. You'll see. Love can work, Philip, if you just let it."

I didn't move.

"I'm not only asking for me. It's for him too. For all of us."

I tried to see her side of it. I tried to understand why it was okay in her mind for all of us all to be together like she wanted. Perhaps it was an invitation to a whole other kind of love, a way of loving which had little to do with possession and need. I tried to see it. But how could I even dream of this. I could not. I knew Silva, she needed Oliver as much as I needed her when I let myself. She was fooling herself to think we could share in any way, this love we each needed so badly. We would only destroy each other in time.

        She rose on her toes and kissed me soft on the lips.

        "You're sure then?"

        I nodded.

        She hesitated, then took a step away.

        "Okay then, stay here alone, with her," she said looking around at the empty room. She bent to pick up her shoes and then walked to the front door. She opened it, sending a cold rush of air along the surface of the old floor. She placed one hand on the doorframe and then slipped her shoes on. When she turned around to look at me, her face and eyes were all in shadow.

        "Then this is how you want it, Philip."

        "Yes," I said

        "Well, I suppose it's time you knew then. Oliver and I have always been lovers."

        I said nothing.

        "I knew you'd take it well, Philip."

        Still, I said nothing. She put her hand on the doorknob.

        "Good bye, Philip," she said, and there was a coldness in her voice, as if she had wanted to say those words long ago. Then she was gone.

        I walked to the window where I could see the jeep and the night around it pulsing with sad expectation. They were going nowhere and would not find him. I could feel it in my bones. The jeep windows were like empty black eyes, the warm exhaust, white and ghostly, floated out behind in the chill air. I watched her walk away, she opened the jeep door and then she was in and gone forever in a matter of seconds.

I waited by the window, watching. It was cold out there. I wondered why I had stayed, alone, in an empty house. I wondered why I was not willing to risk my heart for the chance of real love with them both. But I knew why, I knew her, and myself. We both believed, in the end, that someone had to win and someone lose.

∆ ∆ ∆

After Silva left I warmed some milk to drink and went to bed. I assumed I would never see either of them again. I had decided on my course.

Later, I awoke to a sound in the house, the squeak of the stairs perhaps. Then I saw him--Oliver--in the doorway, alone. He floated toward me like in a dream. I was in my bed, only a blanket and sheet between us.

Against the wall behind him I saw a small canvas, three feet tall, covered in the slashes of an artist gone insane; greens, blues, a storm of red.

"I am going to paint you Philip like it or not, if it's the last thing I ever do" he said, staring down at me from above. He lit a clove and went to the canvas. I could not move, or just didn't. I am not sure which.

As he began to paint he told me about the years he had vanished from us, and of how he had traveled the country and visited the hospitals where they were dying, the ones like him, he said, but worse. He had visited as many as he could, painted their suffering, and learned from some of the wisest of them why it was that they, and he, too, had taken on this angel of death. And on one day, just a few hours before she died, he had seen something in the eyes of a little girl, something that helped him understand why he was there with her. "There is no I Philip, there is only We," he said, "And I was there to remind her of that, so she would not fear death."

I found I couldn't speak. I feared if I broke it he would leave me forever. I didn't understand what he was talking about either, but I listened anyway.

"Now, close your eyes. While I paint, close your eyes," he said and just listen to your heart.

I didn't. He walked toward me. Like a child confronted by a monster I pulled the sheet up to my neck. He came around the side of the bed and sat down like a parent might. He reached out a paint-covered hand and drew his fingers down the side of my face. I turned my head away, but I felt his knuckles slide down my jawbone, to my neck, slowly, and then quickly to my color bone, like a drop of water. I could feel the blood in my body race to where his hand had been. I tried to close my eyes, but couldn't.     "S h u t your eyes," he whispered. The sweetness of cloves touched at my lungs and eyes. I shut my eyes.

Then, suddenly, I felt the presence of my mother at the foot of the bed and I remembered all at once, the dreams that had come upon me in the river that morning. I remembered also the soft sound that my mother's slippers made on the maple floors as she walked up the stairs and down the hallway on her way to wish me goodnight as a child. I sunk deeper in, and then I was gone into the soft presence that Oliver carried with him like a warm blanket.

Then, with eyes closed, I finally told Oliver about what I remembered of the horrible night that she died and the days that followed, and the nightmares of the accident that never left me.

Oliver went to his canvas to paint all that issued forth from me, and in one long night, he took her from me, and with it, the only true story that I have ever told or ever would.

∆ ∆ ∆

Perhaps, there are some people in this world, who are specifically given to recognize instantly where and how we have been broken, and then, in their own way toil forever afterward to help free ourselves from our wounds.

When I awoke the next morning the light was slanting down through my room, polishing the air with impossible promises. Beside my bed, on the nightstand lay the fabulous egg Oliver had painted for me years before. I hadn't really looked closely at the egg in years and I assumed Oliver had placed it there so I would. I picked it up and held it to the light. I saw the place where the endless snake that wound around the egg had caught and held it's own tail.

Then I heard the front door of the house open and close below. I turned on my side. Outside, it was snowing lightly. A layer of white covered the ground and there, in the drive, was a taxicab. I saw Oliver walk out from the house and into view, down the brick walkway to the cab carrying a canvas. He looked as graceful and beautiful as on the very first day he walked into my life.

Inside the cab I saw Silva. She was looking up at him, and for perhaps a second, I thought, at the house. I held the delicate egg in my hand watching the last of the love I had held onto longest being taken away forever. I sat up on the edge of the bed. I watched as the cab drove to the end of the drive, turned left and headed down Main Street.

Δ  Δ  Δ

It was four days later when it appeared in the Living Arts section of the <u>New York Times</u>. I looked on the off chance Oliver's show had been covered. I was at home, by the fire, drinking my morning coffee. Outside the ground was soft. I had decided not to go down to the show. Once I began to read the article I knew we were all finally going over the edge, into the future prepared for us, the one which Oliver had known all along was out there. Maybe on one level, I never actually believed it would happen. Oliver Boswell, the painter and vagabond-prophet was famous, and really dying.

I asked myself how I could not have known the truth? I dropped the paper on my lap after reading the words over and over ten times to be sure. There it was in ink. Oliver was dying. Dying from a virus contracted during his hospitalization in the Westfall hospital four years earlier. All his art work, all along, had been about the millions around the world who carried the same virus and were still as doomed as he, and dying all the time. It was a truth he had hidden from almost everyone until the end. I looked into the fire. Even Claudia had known. She had seen it immediately on the night he arrived at my doorstep looking so ill, and I had refused to listen. I had refused to see.

That day I went for the longest run of my life. I tried to run the guilt out of my blood. While I was running Silva called and left a long message. She said Oliver was gone, as expected, and that now, like everyone else, I must know the truth she had wanted to tell me all along but could not. He wouldn't let me tell you, she said. He said you would blame yourself for his illness but he never said why, not until before he left Philip.

"Please come down her, Philip. I know you didn't mean to hurt him. I forgive you Philip, and he never even blamed you. Please come. I know it wasn't your fault, none of it. He said he pushed you. He said it was his own fault for thinking he could make you let go and that he could set you free before it was time. He was the one who sent me away that night Philip after I climbed the fire escape to your room and we were all going to paint together. He said it was a night just for you and he. So I left. I never should have left you two alone. He said it was his lesson in hubris Philip, and that it set him free from himself in the end. Please come Philip. I leave in two days for Spain. Come with me Philip, it's what he said he wanted for us both, for us to be together once he was gone."

I listened to the message seven times. I listened until I was numb from it. I couldn't decide what to do. Oliver was gone forever now. How could she ever love me?

Δ   Δ   Δ

I arrived in New York three days later. At the gallery there was a long line of people waiting to get in. I cued up and mixed with an assortment of New Yorkers and out of town people. In this very long line of people waiting I could see some who looked like they might not even survive the season.

A middle-aged woman, a line monitor, who reminded me of Carina with her plump face and long hair in a bun, was walking up and down the sidewalk. She looked at me as she went by. I didn't respond. Then on her way back she looked again, a little too long this time. Then she asked my name, wrote it down quickly and disappeared inside. Just about when I had forgotten her altogether I saw her hurrying down the line towards me. I tried to hide myself awhile but she knew what she was about.

"Mr. Abernathy?" She said.

I stepped forward.

"I would like to personally invite you in. We were hoping you would come.

"You were?"

"Yes, we have been expecting you."

She took my arm and ushered me to the front of the line. She led me inside the door and then up a flight of stairs. I made some small talk to try and empty the silence.

"How has the show done?"

"Very well sir. The paintings have all sold."

"All of them?"

"All in the first three days sir."

"Did you get a chance to meet the artist?"

"Mr. Boswell, yes. I helped him hang the paintings, but he only stayed for the opening day. Then he just seemed to disappear. No one seems to know where he went: Very unusual."

"And his sister?"

"Ms. Boswell? She stayed the first few days. She seemed to be waiting for him to return. She flew out to Spain two days ago."

She led me down a hallway and then through another set of doors. I asked her why she was doing this for me.

"It was how Mr. Boswell wanted it, Sir," she said. "He said specifically that you should be treated like his..."

"Like what?"

"His lover, sir."

I stopped in my tracks at the entrance to the show.

"He said that?"

"Yes, he did. You are the one he spoke of, aren't you?"

I looked ahead into the gallery where Oliver waited for me on the walls.

"Yes, I am."

Δ Δ Δ

The gallery was one long hallway with seven open doors to the right. In the first three rooms I found myself surrounded by the portraits of the many dying people Oliver had drawn over the last three years. In the fourth and fifth rooms came the paintings. The dead were hidden under the abstracted oil forms. What was revealed was Oliver's vision of their souls.

I came to the sixth room. It was partitioned. The first was an abstract painting titled "Silva." I knew her from the many spirals of red, green, and blue which swirled like cyclones over the canvas.

Then, when I turned the corner, I faced him, Oliver, in his last self-portrait. It was a simple work. A single large carnelian circle, and inside, the darkness. It took me a moment to see what it was that he had painted. He had captured the exact color, the depth and light of his own lost eye. To me it looked like an explosion of some far off star or world. The kind of thing no human eye is supposed to survive witnessing. But I stood and looked into his eye longer than I ever had before. I wondered if Oliver could feel me looking at him at that very moment. If anyone could do such a thing, it would have been Oliver. I reached out my hand to touch the center of the darkness, where I knew he was heading. But I didn't touch him. I pulled my fingers back. I sensed somehow, that we was already gone. I turned away.

When I entered the last room I saw it, hanging alone, the painting. It was the last dream we had almost never finished. He had completed it. In the end, he hadn't covered over a single inch of my life. It was a perfectly realistic painting, in the background was my house, cupola and all. In the foreground was my mother, Elise. She was dancing over the watermelon green of our yard, with Oliver as her partner. It was realistic except that Oliver had two perfectly healthy eyes looking out over the shoulder of my mother to see the world with, and the both of them were floating above the ground, as if dancing on an invisible floor set there for them in the open air.  Here, in this last work, all had been restored to life, to how I wished it to be.

I looked at the title card next to the painting.

"The Art of Confession," it said.  "On loan from the Philip Kyle Abernathy collection."

I walked backward until I felt myself bump against a wall. I slid down until I was sitting on the wood floor with my hands on my knees. I closed my eyes, and drew in a deep breath. I imagined I could see Silva in Spain, walking alone along a street in Barcelona, searching for an irretrievable past. For a moment I wanted to be with her more than anything in the world. Then,  I saw that day at Westfall when Oliver and I stood on the grass talking with the head mistress of the Academy, he, holding the dictionary to his chest like an old dog saved from certain death. He had tried to show me the difference between seeing what I wished for, and embracing the truth. I had hurt him for it. For showing me that the only true love I had ever known would always be just beyond my grasp, and impossible to bring back to life, unless I let it go.

I stood up then, when I heard the sound of Oliver's many admirers and friends rising on the stairs below. Down on the street, they had opened the doors to the world.